Praise for Pamela Hines and 7...

"I absolutely love Pastor Pamela Hines! She ha... through her book *A Wife's Prayer*, which wa... ...wives Bible study that I'm involved in. She also served as a keynote speaker for my retreat called Treasure You, where women were touched and inspired by her message on prayer. It was life-changing!"

—*Pat Smith, wife of former NFL star Emmitt Smith*

"Pastor Pamela Hines is a true woman of God you can follow because she leads by example. She exudes godly character and living in every way. Pastor Pam has had a permanent impact on my life primarily because of her unconditional love toward me and everyone I have seen her encounter. The love that she has shown her husband, family, and others is extraordinary—a rare find. If only we all could believe in what she has to say. It is remarkable that everyone gets to experience her counsel, wisdom, experience, and advice in *The Fabric of a Woman: Investing in You—Body, Soul, and Spirit*. Having the book is like having the counsel of a best friend, mother, and spiritual guide all in one at your fingertips. Read this book; use it in your daily living. Any woman who takes her counsel will get more than she expects. Get ready, world; the bona fide woman is back in style!"

—*Twyla Betha, wife of pastor and artist Mason Betha*

"I have known Pamela for over fifteen years. Since that time to the present, she has mirrored the embodiment of Christ and exemplified grace as a wife, patience as a mother, and dedication as a minister of the gospel."

—*Evangelist Louise D. Patterson,*
wife of the late Presiding Bishop Gilbert Earl Patterson,
Church of God in Christ, Inc.

"Pastor Pam has been such a light in my life—she has taught me many things that I never experienced growing up. One thing that stands out above all else is her compassion and heart for God's people. I was never a person who cared that much about anything or anyone. But I have learned, through watching her and through praying, that our goal on this earth is to be like God. Pastor Pam's heart and personality are like none other. I strive every day to have a heart like hers—a heart that is close to God's."

—*Nina Hines, daughter-in-law of Pamela Hines*

"Pam and I have been friends for more than twenty years, and I can remember many of the good times that we have shared. We would meet for coffee most mornings after dropping our children off at KinderCare. That would be our quiet time before starting the day.

"Then there were the times we would drive into Chicago (my hometown), and we would sing along to tapes of our favorite songs. Every time one of us messed up, we would start the song over until we got it perfect, or, should I say, at least got all the words right. So, sometimes, we would play one song over and over again for over ninety miles.

"I also remember when Christian Faith Fellowship was founded; my family and I were among the first to join.

"Pam is a wonderful friend with whom I shared many birthdays, heart-to-heart talks, and countless good times. I can truly say that Pam is a wonderful example of a wife, mother, friend, and, most of all, woman of God."

—*Vonnie Cummings, friend*

THE FABRIC OF A WOMAN

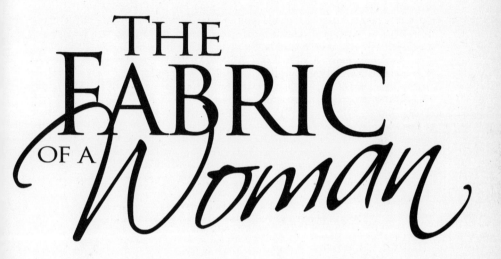

THE FABRIC OF A WOMAN

Investing in You—Body, Soul, and Spirit

PAMELA HINES

WHITAKER
HOUSE

THE FABRIC OF A WOMAN
INVESTING IN YOU—BODY, SOUL, AND SPIRIT
Pamela Hines

ISBN: 978-1-60374-126-2
Printed in the United States of America
© 2009 by Pamela Hines

Whitaker House
1030 Hunt Valley Circle
New Kensington, PA 15068
www.whitakerhouse.com

Library of Congress Cataloging-in-Publication Data

Hines, Pamela, 1961–
  The fabric of a woman / by Pamela Hines.
    p. cm.
  Summary: "Shows women the importance of caring for themselves with such disciplines as prayer, reading the Bible, rest, and healthy lifestyles, allowing God to replenish and restore their bodies, souls, and spirits so that they will be equipped to minister to others"— Provided by publisher.
  ISBN 978-1-60374-126-2 (trade pbk. : alk. paper) 1. Christian women—Religious life. I. Title.
  BV4527.H56 2009
  248.8'43—dc22
                    2009020177

4 5 6 7 8 9 10 11 12 ᴜᴜ 19 18 17 16 15 14 13

This book is dedicated to my mother, Hazel Westmoreland.

FOREWORD

A s I have walked with the Lord for over thirty years, He has brought powerfully anointed people into my life who have strengthened me and my walk with Christ.

When I met Pamela Hines, it was at a time when God was moving me out of my comfort zone into public exposure. My prayer, being a wife and mother on the battlefield, was to be connected to people with a true anointing from God. I was invited to appear on a Christian broadcast, which is where I met her; we were about to share our testimonies with the world. I needed the assurance that the women I came in contact with would be Christians having real relationships with God—true saints who would be there for me. Our meeting was God's purpose.

Pamela has a genuine relationship with our God, and it is made manifest in her lovely countenance and conversation. Her presence so reassured me that I was in God's will. She shared her love for the Lord and for her husband. It was real. It enabled me to connect with her in the spirit.

When I first came to the Lord, a powerful woman of God gave me a book that changed my life. When Pamela gave me her book, I knew I was about to be blessed again. Pamela's book A Wife's Prayer is a powerful daily devotional. I read it every morning, along with other prayer books. Pamela's book changed the way I pray for my husband. Her prayers and knowledge of the Word take us deeper into the dimension of God's truth. She expounds on how to pray effectively according to the Word of God. Her love and reverence for God and His Word is overwhelming. Truly, the Lord has called her into His presence.

As you read *The Fabric of a Woman*, I pray that every fiber of you, as a woman, will be changed. You will learn to take authority over negative thoughts and ungodly appetites, as well as how to pray effectively to get results. Too many saints get caught up in their own bondage. Pamela will help to bring you out. She will take you back to the basics of loving and obeying God's commandments and loving your neighbor as yourself. She really brings it home.

Your sister in Christ,
Shirley T. Gooding
Mother of Cuba Gooding Jr., Academy Award-winning actor

CONTENTS

Preface: The Fabric of Me

For as long as I can remember, I have loved and honored God as my "Abba"—my Daddy. You see, I didn't grow up around my biological father; I have no vivid recollection of him. After my parents separated, we moved away. My mother eventually remarried, but by the time my stepfather became a part of my life, I had already developed a relationship with God the Father, and He has been "Daddy" to me ever since. My stepfather was a wonderful provider who sufficiently supplied everything we stood in need of.

My father-in-law, who has gone home to be with the Lord, also had a great impact on my life. His way with words brought much laughter to my soul, and he was very precious to me. I miss him dearly.

While all of these examples are outstanding, the greatest measure of a father to me is God. As a young child, I was very quiet, reserved, and introverted. But that changed as I grew into the knowledge of who I am in Christ and came to understand that there is a river of life flowing from me, and that I have something valuable to give and to say.

When I accepted Jesus as my personal Savior at eleven years of age, God became Father to me. Embracing the image of who He is to me and who I am in Him has been easy. I trust Him with complete confidence. Every time someone applauds my efforts or accomplishments, I am reminded that He created me in His image. (See Genesis 1:26–27.) He is the One I honor for giving me the person with the greatest, most positive impact on my life: my mother.

I was created by God, *"knit...together in my mother's womb"* (Psalm 139:13 NIV), and He knew what He was doing when He chose Hazel Westmoreland to be my mother. When someone says that I'm like my mother, it gives me great pleasure. If I can be even half the woman my mother was, it will be an honor of the highest distinction. She was truly a special lady, beautiful on both the outside and inside. I imagine that any woman who has or had a good relationship with her mother believes the same thing.

"Doll Baby" is what she was called as a child. The thick, curly locks that adorned her head, the chocolate brown skin that covered her body, and the words of comfort that flowed frequently from her lips reflected the beauty of her countenance and the sweetness of her temperament. As a woman, she was poised and feminine, yet confident and strong. She wasn't cantankerous or argumentative. Her words were always seasoned with grace, so they ministered that same grace to the hearer.

The truth is, I can hardly think about myself without thinking about my mother. My most prominent characteristics and tendencies are a tribute to her example. So, if I seem patient, kind, loving, and trusting, it is because the fabric of my temperament was woven by the Designer's finest thread, just as my mother's was. If ever there was a person fashioned in the image and likeness of God, it was my mother. She was the epitome of a giver—she gave of her resources, her substance, her worth, and her life. It didn't matter who you were or what you did; if you needed someone to minister to your success, my mother was the woman for the job.

My heart for giving and helping people to excel flows from what I observed my mother doing. It was my mother whom I studied reverently, for she portrayed the image of God in every aspect of her life. I thank God for that attribute: the power and the willingness to give. I have honored God in my giving, and He has blessed me in every aspect of my life—spirit, soul, and body.

My mother received salvation late in her life, but the godly traits that she exhibited are evident in the lives of me and my two sisters, LaVander and Ruby. God knit my mother together with the necessary threads to produce a rich fabric that would flow to every one of her descendants. My mother left a legacy that was instilled in us as we observed her. She didn't sit down with us and say, "Let me teach this to you"; we learned the importance of giving by the precepts she demonstrated and the example of her steadfast nature.

Every woman is not so fortunate to have had someone, particularly a mother, who offers her such opportunity and privilege. That's when you have to allow the Holy Spirit to begin to design you in the image of God the Father. If you've never had a godly example to follow—no mentor or confidant to nurture your worth or establish and affirm your footing as a child of God—then God has made Himself available to you in order to fashion you in His likeness. If you think it's too late to learn of God and follow His example, it's not. You're not too old; you haven't gone so far as to travel beyond God's grace, for it is immeasurable. His grace is sufficient for you, but you have to trust Him. You have to believe that He is able, willing, *and* available to do exceeding, abundantly above all that you ask or could even imagine, according to *His* power that works in you! (See Ephesians 3:20.) Never forget that you are *"fearfully and wonderfully made"* (Psalm 139:14).

God bless you,
Pamela

INTRODUCTION

There is an underlying fabric to all of us as women—a common manner in which every aspect of who we are functions and operates. The fabric of you is who you are; it's what makes you, you. Through your fabric—your unique makeup—you touch the world; you commune with God; you love, feel, and understand.

We have been *"fearfully and wonderfully made"* (Psalm 139:14). This means that we have been crafted by a loving Creator who endued each of us with a marvelous and unique set of attributes, skills, and talents that compose the fabric of our lives.

Clothing manufacturers use many types of fabric: silk, cotton, polyester, nylon, wool, and the list goes on. Silk is said to be one of the strongest natural fibers in the world, while polyester isn't so famous for its durability. What kind of fabric are you made of? The fabric of a woman is an intricately woven tapestry masterfully crafted with rich hues of virtue, wit, intuition, strength, character, and a host of other fine threads. The fibers of her being define the nature of her spirit, soul, and body. We are much like the exquisitely beautiful and intrinsically valuable natural fabrics; we live, we move, we breathe, and we grow, unlike man-made synthetics.

We would all love to be made from a cut of fabric that is dirt-resistant and flame-retardant; one that never tears or unravels. But the truth of the matter is that life often pulls at our loose threads, threatening to make us fall apart at the seams. Life brings constant pressures that can overwhelm us if we aren't daily cultivating the fabric of our lives. Like God does, we need to invest in who we are and in what we have in order to withstand the pressures of life.

If we fail to invest in ourselves, we will sustain unwanted injuries to our fabric. The good news is that when we walk closely with God, He becomes our Seamster, and He is quick and adept at mending the rips, tears, and loose threads of life.

God is an Investor. He created us to be fruitful—to multiply and replenish. He uses the assets of those who commit to obedient, faith-filled lives to cause the investment to grow or mature, just as a profitable financial investment yields an opportunity to earn income or profit. God's investment in our lives provides wholeness for our entire beings—body, soul, and spirit—so that nothing is missing from or broken in our lives. His objective is to make each aspect of us complete: completely healed, completely whole, completely functional. His investment increases as we continuously attend to and appropriate His Word in our lives. His Word defines our worth because it is the standard for our value.

> *God's Word defines our worth because it is the standard for our value.*

In your life, what's failing? What isn't rising or increasing? As never before, the time has come to recognize your worth and allow the "Great Investor" to develop and heal you. He wants you to see yourself as He does, no longer being hostage to or dependent upon a poor self-image of someone else's opinion about who you are but rather adopting a revelation of who He has created you to be.

1
GOD IS AN INVESTOR

To capitalize on our ability to produce, God continually invests in us. According to 2 Peter 1:3, He has given us *"all things that pertain to life and godliness."* God has invested His attributes in us so that we may have the ability to prosper. When He deposits His nature, character, and ability into us, He expects the return to be people who have been transformed into His image and likeness.

Investing is the action of redirecting resources from being consumed in order to create benefits in the future. The word *create* means to generate, produce, fashion, or construct. Each of these references suggests that if anyone takes the time to create something, he seeks to benefit from its existence, and the best way to maximize the existence of a creation is to invest in and protect it.

As our lives bear fruit, God creates more and more opportunities for us to increase, resulting in the growth of His investment. His plan for us is that we continually produce abundant fruit in our lives. He gives us gifts and talents in order to enhance His ability to gain a greater return, and His ultimate desire is for you to increase in such a way that the fruit of your life draws others to Himself.

In Matthew 25:14–29, Jesus told a wonderful story about a farmer who was a respectable businessman. He said, *"For the kingdom of heaven is like a man traveling to a far country, who called his own servants and delivered his goods to them"* (verse 14). Before the businessman left the country, he gathered his chief financial officers and instructed them to invest his money. To one, he gave five talents; to another, he gave two talents; and to a third man, he gave one talent. Each man received no more than what corresponded to his ability or potential to produce. The man who received the five talents invested them and doubled his assets. Likewise, the man who received two talents invested them, yielding a return of two additional talents. But the man who received one talent hid it.

After a long time, the businessman returned and reconciled the increase with each servant. The first man joyfully reported to his master that the five talents had doubled to ten. His master applauded his employee's faithfulness and gave him a promotion.

The second man told his master that he, too, had received a double return on his investment, and he received a promotion, as well. The businessman said to his employees, "Great job! I appreciate your diligence in getting the job done. Because you have been faithful over these few things, I will make you rulers over many things. Let's celebrate!" (See verses 21, 23.)

Then, the man who had received one talent said, "Sir, I knew you were a harsh man; your investment was yielding a return where you hadn't put it and gaining interest where you hadn't cultivated. I was afraid I would lose your money, so I hid it. But I have it. It's all here. Here's your money back." (See verses 24–25.)

The businessman replied, "That doesn't make sense. If you knew I received a return where I didn't invest it, and that I gained interest where I didn't cultivate, and you thought you would lose the talent, why didn't you deposit my money in the bank? I could have gotten at least some interest on it." He then took the talent from the lazy man and gave it to the first man to add to his ten talents. (See verses 26–28.)

This principle does not apply to money alone. Rather, it touches every area of our lives: our gifts, talents, abilities, resources, spirits, souls, and bodies.

God, our Divine Investor, is a lot like the businessman in this story. He has delegated many gifts, talents, and abilities to us, and He expects that we will remain diligent to increase what He has entrusted to us.

A Faithful Investor

To those who use well what they are given, even more will be given, and they will have abundance. But from those who do nothing, even what little they have will be taken away. (Matthew 25:29 NLT)

In the investment world, if an investment fails to produce, a smart investor pulls out when she sees that the price of her shares is falling. God, on the other hand, is committed to His investment. He will never pull out of your life, but He *will* prune, or cut back, any unproductive areas to ensure that His "stock" does not crash. Jesus said, *"I am the true vine, and My Father is the vinedresser. Every branch in Me that does not bear fruit He takes away; and every branch that bears fruit He prunes, that it may bear more fruit"* (John 15:1–3). He protects His investments because He is a wise and caring Investor.

> *God is committed to His investment. He will never pull out of your life.*

In all His glory, ability, and power, God opened Himself to man. He made us with free will, giving us the privilege to choose and refuse, and this choice includes Him. In His foreknowledge, He knew that we might potentially forsake Him, yet He still chose to make an investment in us, and that investment was the sacrifice of His own Son. Every investment comes at a price, and this one was no different, except in that it was the highest price ever paid. We were bought with the price of the shed blood of Jesus Christ. (See 1 Corinthians 6:20.)

God sent His only Son in exchange for our redemption. As an Investor, God chose to "lend" Jesus (the original good) in exchange for you and me (the yields on His investment). He made an investment of one Son, and that investment split many times over, bringing Him many sons. Hebrews 2:10 says, *"For it was fitting for Him, for whom are all things and by whom are all things, in bringing many sons to glory, to make the captain of their salvation perfect through sufferings."* And among these "sons"—God's children—we women are extremely valuable.

The Value of a Woman

The value of an object is usually determined by what it's made of. For example, I have various jewelry pieces composed of cubic zirconia (CZ) and others of diamond. I treat my diamonds much differently than I do my CZ. My diamonds are kept in a special place, but I may put my CZ on the bathroom counter, in my coat pocket, or at the bottom of my purse. If I lose my CZ, I won't shed a tear; if I lose my diamonds, however, my response will be different. To God, we are more valuable than many diamonds. If we fail to recognize the value God places on us, we will never appreciate our worth as women.

My husband and I built our home, and I was privileged to have the opportunity to customize many of the features. When it came to fabrics, I fell in love with certain textures, colors, and patterns from some of the most exclusive designers in the business. Most of my favorite fabrics were natural, many of them mentioned in the Bible, and I discovered that the finer fabrics where those spun by the designer himself. They had been handcrafted to the designer's specifications. In the same way, God has handcrafted each of us into a unique, vibrant fabric. We were fearfully and wonderfully made, and we bear His image, for He was not ashamed to call us His own. *"I will be their God, and they shall be My people....I will be a Father to you, and you shall be My sons and daughters"* (2 Corinthians 6:16, 18).

> *God has handcrafted each of us into a unique, vibrant fabric.*

Created a Woman

God made us into women. He never makes mistakes; He had no doubts or regrets when He made you and me in His image and likeness. Let's return to the Genesis account for a few highlights. In the first chapter of Genesis, we read that both male and female were created: *"So God created man in His own image; in the image of God He created him; male and female He created them"* (Genesis 1:27). In the second chapter, we learn the details of how God made both genders. The male was made, or formed, from the dust of the ground (see Genesis 2:7), and the female was made from a rib that was taken from man.

> *The LORD God caused a deep sleep to fall on Adam, and he slept; and He took one of his ribs, and closed up the flesh in its place. Then the rib which the Lord God had taken from man He made into a woman, and He brought her to the man. And Adam said: "This is now bone of my bones and flesh of my flesh; she shall be called Woman, because she was taken out of Man."* (Genesis 2:21–23)

A creation is something unique that would not naturally occur on its own; rather, it depends on the initiative and action of a creator.

It was the breath of God that created man and woman in the beginning. But their bodies were made from what already existed in the earth. God's purpose for creating Eve is found in Genesis 2:18: *"And the LORD God said, 'It is not good that man should be alone; I will make him a helper comparable to him.'"*

Until God formed Eve's body and brought her to life, there was no suitable companion for Adam in the earth. Every animal of the field, fish in the sea, and bird in the air had a companion, but there was none for man. God, the Great Physician, is naturally an unparalleled anesthesiologist. He caused a deep sleep to come upon Adam, and then, as Adam slept, He accurately and precisely removed one of his ribs, using it to form woman.

Created for a Unique Purpose

While man was formed from the dust of the ground, woman was made from the rib of the man. We women are strong because we're made from strong stuff. The ribs serve several important purposes in the body: they protect vital organs, such as the heart and lungs, and they aid in breathing—when you inhale, they move up to enable your lungs to expand, and when you exhale, they move down to push the air from your lungs.

Likewise, woman serves an important purpose on the earth. She was ordained by God to be a helper, a nurturer, and an influencer. Her role on the earth is distinctly different from the role of man. As women, we possess great power and ability. Satan understood the unique power and influence of women. For this reason, he chose to speak with Eve in the form of a serpent in the garden of Eden. (See Genesis 3:1–6.) He knew that, once tempted, she would carry her influence to tempt Adam, as well. Through the woman, Satan succeeded in getting Adam to defy God's orders.

God wants us to use our influence as women to further His purposes on the earth. We must not heed the voice of the enemy, who still tries to manipulate the influence of women, for to do so would contradict the plan of God and consequently disqualify us from living in God's blessing. Women who choose to obey the voice of God will always have God's best operating in their lives. Use your influence as a woman to bring forth life—not just in a literal sense, but in every arena in which you find yourself, because that's what you were made to do.

> *Use your influence as a woman to bring forth life, because that's what you were made to do.*

2

INVEST IN YOURSELF

Unfortunately, many women sacrifice their personal care, growth, or development because they devote all of their time and efforts to serving others. Serving others is important, of course; we're called to do so as a way of administering the grace of God (see 1 Peter 4:10) and as an expression of worship (see Hebrews 13:16). But how can we really give ourselves to our families, and to others who depend on us, if we fail to first take the time to get what we need?

In order to bless someone, you must have something to bless with, something to give. It is important that you, as a woman, recognize that your greatest need is to connect with God, thereby receiving all that He has to give you and also giving your best to others. When we connect with God, He fills our spirit lives with His life, and His life enables us to accomplish all that we are responsible to do. God becomes the Source; we become resources. He is the primary Depositor, the Source of our supply.

What do you have to give others? What is in your account to give your husband, your children, your job, your relationships, and so on? Every time we give of ourselves in these various areas, we are depleting our own accounts. This is the importance of continuously connecting with God and receiving all that He has to give. When we draw from Him, He renews us continuously.

When we don't take adequate care of ourselves, we hinder God's ability to be who He truly wants to be in our lives. It reveals that we place little value on how we have been fashioned and who God has made us to be. We can't be effective or successful at taking care of others if we neglect to take care of ourselves.

Unless we invest in our bodies, souls, and spirits, we will begin to express on the outside the turmoil we feel inwardly. Some women seek attention because they were deprived of it at some point in their lives, perhaps as children. People sometimes express internal hurt and scream out for attention in the way they walk, talk, and dress. Exaggerated outward expressions are usually manifestations of the insecurities we hold in our-

A woman of excellence takes care of herself.

selves. When we invest in ourselves, we can become the women of God He purposed us to be. But if we fail to invest in our bodies, souls, and spirits, then the flesh takes the liberty of coloring our personas to reflect an image other than the ones God designed. A woman of excellence takes care of herself. Don't take care of everybody else and fail to take care of yourself.

Reaching the End of Your Rope

If you're living in a place of irritation or frustration, you may blame others, but in most cases, frustration and fatigue are linked to your own failure to invest in yourself. Many women reach the ends of their ropes because they are weighed down by their daily routines. Chauffeuring children to dance lessons and soccer practice, serving on the Parent Teacher Association, keeping up with the laundry, washing the dishes, shopping for groceries...the to-do lists of most women go on and on. But the end of your rope is exactly where you need to be. For when you have reached the end of your rope, which represents your own strength and personal efforts, you can grab ahold of God's rope instead. His rope is infinitely stronger than yours, and it has a sustaining power to help you with your day-to-day tasks and challenges. His rope is a cord of three strands—Father, Son, and Holy Spirit—and *"a cord of three strands is not quickly torn apart"* (Ecclesiastes 4:12 NASB).

Many of us are trying to do everything in our own strength, only to find that our strength has limitations. God's strength, on the other hand, is limitless. *"The* LORD *is the strength of my life"* (Psalm 27:1). *"In God is my salvation and my glory; the rock of my strength, and my refuge, is in God"* (Psalm 62:7). But it must be understood that we are strong only *"in the Lord and in the power of His might"* (Ephesians 6:10). Our strength comes from God, and our strength is in Him.

Renewing Yourself Renews Others

As a woman, a wife, and a mother, I know firsthand the value of spending time investing in myself. Through the Word of God and the guidance of the Holy Spirit, I have learned how to minister to and invest in myself so that I can be all that I need to be for my husband and children.

If we commit to taking time to pour refreshment and renewal into our own lives on a consistent basis, it will eliminate much of the irritation and many of the frustrations that countless women are living with, day after day. We shouldn't look run-down or feel years older than we are because we've given until there is nothing left of us to give. I don't believe that God expects us to maintain healthy families or prosperous businesses only to lose our own health, energy, and identities in the process.

Your body is a temple of the Holy Spirit (see 1 Corinthians 3:16), and God expects you to take care of His dwelling place. In Matthew 22:37–39, Jesus identified the two principal commandments: 1) love God with all your heart, soul, and mind; and 2) love your neighbor *as you love yourself.* Most people focus on that verse's directive to love their neighbors but ignore the instruction to love themselves. Loving oneself and loving one's neighbor are equally important parts of that greatest commandment, but for so many years, we have failed to realize it. Every day of your life, you are required to invest in something or someone. So, why not invest in you? It all comes down to loving yourself enough not to overlook yourself.

> *Every day of your life, you are required to invest in something or someone. So, why not invest in you?*

In Romans 12:3, Paul said that we are *"not to think of* [ourselves] *more highly than* [we] *ought to think, but to think soberly, as God has dealt to each one a measure of faith."* The point isn't that we are not to think highly of ourselves; rather, we are not to think *too highly* of ourselves. Never underestimate your value. The Creator of the universe fashioned you to be a unique person, and His immeasurable love gives you matchless worth. To think highly of yourself simply means to add yourself to your priority list.

We understand the need to invest in our relationships in order to make them solid and strong. But what about ourselves? What about you? When was the last time you pampered yourself? How long has it been since your last vacation? It's time to stop waiting for Calgon to take you away and to book the plane ticket yourself. When was the last time you invested in you?

3

THE FABRIC OF YOU

When you take the time to invest in yourself, you strengthen the fabric of your life. Silk is said to be one of the strongest natural fibers in the world, dating back to 3000 BC in China. Because of its internal properties, silk will retain its shape, even if stretched; it's stretch resistant. Polyester, on the other hand, is not a natural fabric. It's a synthetic material that is not breathable, and, once stained, polyester is difficult to clean.

The fabric of our lives is strong and durable, designed by God to last. We were cut from the fabric of God. We were made to withstand opposition, stains, and tears. Every part of who we are is expected to endure under pressure, by the grace of God. Life does pull at us; it brings pressures and challenges that can be overwhelming. The key to having a life that's pressure resistant is practicing daily submission to the Word of God, as well as having regular fellowship with God Himself, reading His Word, praying, and basking in His presence. When you spend time with God, you are cultivating the fabric of your life and preserving its longevity and strength. By submitting yourself to God, you are able to resist the devil, causing him to flee. (See James 4:7.)

Fabric that has been torn may require more than a few stitches. In some cases, it may never be restored to its original form; however, it can be reshaped or remade into something new. And isn't that just what God does with us? When the challenges and toils of life rip gaping holes in the fabric of our lives, our Designer allows nothing to go to waste. He sees the potential in everything, and He will reshape, restore, and renew us until we are returned to a place of beauty, purpose, and value. He gives us *"beauty for ashes, the oil of joy for mourning, the garment of praise for the spirit of heaviness; that [we] may be called trees of righteousness, the planting of the* LORD, *that He may be glorified"* (Isaiah 61:3).

Often, our challenge is getting through the process of being reshaped and restored. We may experience pain as we let go of who we used to be or as God recreates us. Allowing Him to do so requires incredible patience and an unyielding trust in Him. It can be difficult to meet these requirements, but the challenge is entirely worth it, for He will mend the flaws in our fabric and complete His work in us. We can have the assurance of Paul, who wrote, *"I am confident of this very thing, that He who began a good work in you will perfect it until the day of Christ Jesus"* (Philippians 1:6 NASB).

> *Fellowshipping with the Father is one of the many ways in which we invest in ourselves.*

Our heavenly Father desires the members of His body, the church, to be spotless and blameless, a state that can be achieved only through justification by the blood of Jesus Christ. He loves the church so much that He...

...gave Himself for her, that He might sanctify and cleanse her with the washing of water and by the word, that He might present her to Himself a glorious church, not having spot or wrinkle or any such thing, but that she should be holy and without blemish.

(Ephesians 5:25–27)

In order to refine our resilience and withstand the many pressures of life, it is essential that we invest in who we are, as well as in what we have—in Christ Jesus. Fellowshipping with the Father is one of the many ways in which we invest in ourselves.

Removing the Stains of Life

As we have noted, there are many things that can weaken the fabric of our lives, causing stains, rips, and tears to discolor or wear at our beings. A stain is a discoloration caused by a foreign substance that penetrates the fibers of a fabric. To remove a stain, you don't rub it; the proper technique is to blot it. Blotting applies pressure to the stain and absorbs the pigment.

We, too, require blotting from time to time. When we suffer stains, the blotting cloth of God's tender mercies applies healing pressure to the fabric of our lives. But if you try rubbing out the stain on your own, you will only cause smearing, further damaging your fabric.

God absorbs the stains of our lives—those dark, depressing areas that bring hurt and discomfort. To *blot out* is to make indistinguishable, to cover up entirely, to present as if it had never existed. More important, God blots out our sins, which are stains with eternal impact. Psalm 51:1 says, *"Have mercy upon me, O God, according to Your lovingkindness; according unto the multitude of Your tender mercies,* **blot out** *my transgressions"* (emphasis added).

> *God absorbs the stains of our lives—those dark, depressing areas that bring hurt and discomfort.*

When God blots out our transgressions, we become justified, "just-as-if-I'd" never sinned. We have this assurance in Isaiah 1:18: *"Though your* **sins are like scarlet***, they shall be as* **white as snow***; though they are* **red like crimson***, they shall be as* **wool***"* (emphasis added). God removes the glaring scarlet of our sins, purifying our lives' fabric and making it righteous and free. When God cleanses our lives of sins and stains, He does so with the greatest love and care.

4

A TRIUNE BLEND OF FABRICS

B ecause we were created in the image and likeness of God (see Genesis 1:26), who is a Trinity, we, too, are triune. Each of us comprises three main components: body, soul, and spirit. Of these components, your spirit is the essence of who you are. Your spirit is the part of you that is endued with life; it's the part of you that continues to be, even when your soul vegetates and your breath has left your body. It is your spirit that affords you the privilege of spending eternity in heaven if you have accepted Christ as your Lord and Savior. It's the quintessence of who you are; it's your core, your fundamental nature.

To be viable on the earth, however, we require the personality and creativity of our souls and the fiber and flexibility of our bodies. If one measure of our being ceases to function, we are rendered incomplete. A Hebrew scholar once remarked that in Hebrew, the word for *likeness* means "an exact duplication in kind." I believe that to be true. There are three major components of God, and there are likewise three major components of you. Just as God the Father would never neglect the Son or the Holy Spirit, neither should you neglect any part of who you are. God lives through each part of the Trinity, and we have to allow Him to release His life into us by investing in every part of our "tri-unity."

You are a spirit.

Your spirit is the core of who you are. It is the fundamental likeness of God that gives life to your physical body.

+ *"There is a spirit in man, and the breath of the Almighty gives him understanding"* (Job 32:8).

+ *"The spirit of a man is the lamp of the LORD, searching all the inner depths of his heart"* (Proverbs 20:27).

You possess a soul.

Your soul is the seat of your emotions and decisions; it comprises your mind, your will, and your intellect.

+ *"And man became a living soul"* (Genesis 2:7 KJV).

+ *"Bless the LORD, O my soul; and all that is within me, bless His holy name!"* (Psalm 103:1).

You live in a physical body.

Your body is the vehicle that gives you access to the earth and mobility within it.

+ *"Didn't you realize that your body is a sacred place, the place of the Holy Spirit? Don't you see that you can't live however you please, squandering what God paid such a high price for?"* (1 Corinthians 6:19–20 MSG).

+ *"So we make it our goal to please him, whether we are at home in the body or away from it"* (2 Corinthians 5:9 NIV).

Complete and Whole

*Now may the God of peace Himself sanctify you completely; and may your whole **spirit, soul, and body be preserved blameless** at the coming of our Lord Jesus Christ.*

(1 Thessalonians 5:23, emphasis added)

This verse is an excellent revelation of God's heart, describing how valuable you are to Him. Notice that it says, *"your whole spirit and soul and body"*—not someone else's, but your own. This validates the idea that God wants you to be taken care of, as we previously discussed.

The apostle Paul was praying that the people in Thessalonica would be *"preserved blameless."* It's hard to understand exactly what was being communicated without investigating the roots of the words used in this passage. The word *preserved* comes from a word that means "to attend to carefully, to take care of, and to guard." The word *blameless* means "without fault or defect."

In essence, Paul's prayer was that your whole spirit, soul, and body be guarded and attended to carefully, without any defects. It is significant to note that Paul qualified the amount of time God desires for you to live in this flawless, perfect state: *"until our Lord Jesus Christ comes again"* (1 Thessalonians 5:23 NLT). God desires us to take care to preserve our beings for the rest of our lives.

> *God desires us to take care to preserve our beings for the rest of our lives.*

The Word of God is the revealed will of God, and if God wanted the people in Thessalonica to be preserved, spirit, soul, and body, He wants the same for the entire church today, because God shows no partiality. (See Acts 10:34.)

Know what God's Word says about you, then look in the mirror to assess your spirit, soul, and body. What's out of place? What needs to be mended? It is time for us to be healed. No longer must we depend on the reflection of someone else's image or another person's perception of who we are. Nor should we allow a poor self-image to dictate our worth and minimize our value. The true essence of who we really are is who God created us to be. Our bodies, souls, and spirits are made in God's image, and it's up to us to invest in them.

INVESTING IN YOUR BODY

INVESTING IN YOUR BODY

The apostle Paul compared our physical bodies to *"jars of clay"* in which we *"always carry around...the death of Jesus, so that the life of Jesus may also be revealed"* (2 Corinthians 4:7, 10 NIV). As a believer, you inhabit a physical body designed by God to be a container and transporter of Christ in the earth. God designed your body for His exact purpose. *"Your body is the temple of the Holy Spirit who is in you, whom you have from God, and you are not your own...you were bought with a price"* (1 Corinthians 6:19–20).

Although his spirit was preexistent in the plan of God, Adam, the first man, did not exist until God made his body from the dust of the ground. When Adam was formed, his body was lifeless—that is, until God *"breathed into his nostrils the breath of life"* (Genesis 2:7). When God breathed into Adam's nostrils, he came alive. It took the life within God to give life to Adam's physical body.

Absent of our spirits, we're mere formations of clay. However, God has an expectation that we will do all that we can to properly maintain our bodies while on the earth. Your body plays an important role in the plan of God, and it needs special attention and care.

The body is a communicator, and it does not lie. Whether it's cared for or neglected is revealed both inside and out. The proper care of your body is essential to optimal health and longevity, and it also brings honor and glory to God.

Many years ago, along with pastoring, I became a certified Image Consultant. I did so in hopes of helping to educate women in the areas of health, nutrition, fashion, and skin and body care. Immediately after being certified, I established what I called The Women's Image Course, a series of lessons designed to unlock the unique potential in the lives of women. I traveled and shared what I had learned, and I was extremely blessed by the countless women who responded to and were affected by the information. I encountered more than a few women who had never learned the basics of caring for themselves. My goal was not to make them imitations of me but rather to give them the necessary tools to be their absolute best. Within a short period of time, the demand for the information grew, and in our church alone I could see the positive impact that these teachings had on the women in our congregation.

I want to explore the proper care and maintenance of the body so that you can live a fulfilling life now. To begin, making yourself a priority is essential as well as having a routine that is practical for use in your daily life.

Our perception of beauty seems to focus more on the visible attributes of the body than the invisible. Psalm 149:4 says, *"The Lord takes pleasure in His people; He will beautify the humble with salvation."* Real beauty does not reside on the surface; it emanates from a woman's inner being. Her appearance reflects who she is inside, and her actions are an extension of her being. She connects with her inner beauty not by trying to be beautiful but by believing that she is fashioned in the beauty of God's holiness.

In this section, I would like for you to see the importance of total body care, including a proper diet, regular exercise, rest and relaxation, and skincare. From our heads to our toes, we need to be whole, with nothing out of sync. We should strive to have beautiful hair and proper blood sugar levels.

5

GOD LIVES HERE

Do you not know that your body is a temple of the Holy Spirit, who is in you, whom you have received from God? You are not your own; you were bought at a price. Therefore honor God with your body.
—1 Corinthians 6:19–20 (NIV)

Survival is the body's most important business, but the body's ability to operate as God designed it to changes as we age. Throughout childhood, our bodies increase their functionality, adding new capabilities and processes. This continues until the point at which the opposite occurs—we begin to lose functionality as we reach old age. Eyesight may worsen, comprehension may dim, joints may stiffen, and the body starts to lose functionality.

The physical and mental deterioration that accompanies age was not God's original intent for us. But ever since humankind's first act of sinful disobedience, and the resulting inevitability of physical death, a decline in bodily functions and a loss of youth have been facts of human existence.

Death may be inevitable, but the types of deterioration we experience as we come closer to it don't have to be. Many of the ailments and diseases that plague the human body are consequences of our own lifestyles; what we choose to eat, how much we choose to drink, how often we exercise, and other factors can help us evade certain problems—or can deliver us right into their clutches. Our health often comes down to our consumption. For instance, consuming excessive quantities of red meat may lead to heart disease. Unhealthy practices, such as drinking significant amounts

> *The essence of the lives we lived as young women should be in full bloom by the time we advance into maturity.*

of alcohol on a regular basis, may ruin our livers with cirrhosis; smoking cigarettes may invite emphysema or lung cancer. And the list goes on.

Our bodies are temples of the Holy Spirit. (See 1 Corinthians 3:16.) If we don't take care of them, no matter how spiritual we are, they will cease to function. We thank God for doctors and for medical breakthroughs, but His desire is for us to live in divine health. Each of us has only one life, only one body; if we don't give it the nutrients, rest, and vigorous exercise it requires, we may shorten what could have been a longer life. When we reach our senior years, life should still be flowing from us like beautiful, colorful garments. The essence of the lives we lived as young women should be in full bloom by the time we advance into maturity. We should be radiant and full of life, love, and the peace of God.

Ageless Beauty

God created us to have long lives. (See Psalm 91:16.) He created us to live life to the fullest. (See John 10:10.) We marvel at anyone who lives longer than a century, even as many of us hope to do so ourselves. But did you realize that many people from Bible times lived for hundreds of years?

I do believe that God wants us to get better as we age. Sarah, the wife of Abraham, was sixty-five years old when Pharaoh noticed her beauty and wanted to take her as his wife. (See Genesis 12:14–15.) Years later, when Sarah was even older, King Abimelech of Gerar saw her, and he, too, wanted her as his wife. But God appeared to him in a dream, demanding that he let her go because she was Abraham's wife. (See Genesis 20:1–3.)

My point is that even when Sarah was well into her eighties, men were still overwhelmed by her beauty. She had a husband, a son, and the responsibilities of a wife and mother, just like we do. But she lived in a covenant of obedience to God, and, as a result, she reaped the benefit of ageless beauty.

The same blessing that Sarah walked in is available to us today. Hebrews 8:6 states that we have an even better covenant in the Abrahamic covenant, which is established upon better promises. The blessing of ageless beauty is ours. Psalm 149:4 says that God will *"beautify the humble with salvation."* Salvation is a work of the heart that produces a beauty that manifests in our physical bodies.

> *Salvation is a work of the heart that produces a beauty that manifests in our physical bodies.*

As we mature in age, our lives should still reflect a vibrant spirit, a lively mind, and a healthy body. God wants us to be vivacious and graceful no matter our ages. Expect Him to satisfy your mouth with good things so that your youth is renewed like the eagle, as He promises to do in Psalm 103:5. Expect to get better with age and purpose to walk in divine health. If God can transform our minds, based on Romans 12:2, He can also enliven our physical bodies. As Paul wrote in Romans 8:11,

> *If the Spirit of Him who raised Jesus from the dead dwells in you, He who raised Christ from the dead will also give life to your mortal bodies through His Spirit who dwells in you.*

As a woman of God, you should be better at forty than you were at thirty and better at sixty than you were at fifty. God wants us to be vivacious and graceful, no matter our ages. And, although some may disagree, I believe we can become increasingly beautiful as we age and develop deeper spiritual maturity. But this type of beauty comes only when we truly walk with God, invest in ourselves, and take advantage of the blessings He has to offer us.

God wants His *zoë*—the Greek term for His full, abundant life—to permeate your being. He doesn't want the circumstances of life to overwhelm you and steal from you His joy, peace, and rest. The Bible says that Moses died at 120 years of age, and even then, *"his eyes were not dim nor his natural vigor diminished"* (Deuteronomy 34:7). *The Message* Bible puts it this way: *"His eyesight was sharp; he still walked with a spring in his step"* (emphasis added). That is what I'm talking about—walking with God and investing in your life so that, just prior to death, you still have a spring in your step.

Moses was a man who spent a considerable amount of time in the presence of God, and because he was committed to spending time with God in fellowship—one way of investing in himself—the Bible says that the skin of his face shone so brightly that he had to cover it when talking with people. (See Exodus 34:35.) After his first encounter with God on Mount Sinai, Moses spent the rest of his life living in communion with God and ministering to God's people. And how he spent the majority of his time—basking in God's presence—was revealed on his face. This is a powerful truth that I believe every woman needs to grasp.

6

Diet: A Balancing Act

Ask any woman to name one thing she is tempted to obsess about, and she will probably say her weight. Many of us struggle constantly with weight; if we're not too fat, then we're too skinny. From eating disorders such as anorexia nervosa to weight issues such as obesity, problems with weight are prevalent among American women, and they're starting earlier and earlier; between 1980 and 2007, the number of obese children between six and nine years of age tripled, according to the Centers for Disease Control and Prevention. And the United States Department for Health and Human Services predicts that overweight adolescents have a 70 percent chance of becoming overweight or obese adults.

Like many women, I have experienced a struggle with my weight. There was a time in my life when my appetite was greatly suppressed. Rather than viewing food as essential nourishment, I viewed it as my enemy, and I refused to eat. Stress made me even less inclined to eat, and I lost a significant amount of weight. (Some people do the opposite: they eat more under stress. Excessive stress seems to either compel us to overeat or restrain us from eating at all.) I was never clinically diagnosed with anorexia nervosa, but my husband saw my condition and prayed for me.

As a young wife, I had to care for my husband after he was struck by lightning. He needed time to recover, and it was a while before he could return to work. We also had two sons, one of whom was seriously ill. I had to balance supporting my husband, caring for my sons, and taking care of our home as my husband recuperated from his traumatic experience.

Did I mention that I was also attending school and working to make ends meet? We had no car at our disposal, so we had to rely on borrowed vehicles for transportation, and we had outstanding medical bills. My load of responsibilities started to take a toll on me, and it was manifested as stress. There was entirely too much going on at one time for me to keep up.

Through prayer and consistency, I began to change my thoughts about food, and it changed my life. Now, I intentionally make time to eat right, exercise, and drink plenty of water, all of which help to balance my body so that I don't gain or lose excessive weight. I have the necessary energy and stamina to pursue whatever God has planned for me on any given day, and because I have learned to cast my cares upon Him (see 1 Peter 5:7), I know that I won't become stressed and worn out.

Food: Friend or Foe?

All the labor of man is for his mouth, and yet the soul is not satisfied.
(Ecclesiastes 6:7)

One can be overweight and still be starved for nutrients.

Once, when I was praying, the Lord revealed to me that His people are not eating right spiritually, just as they aren't eating right naturally. Living in one of the most *overfed* and yet *undernourished* nations of the world, one-third of Americans are seriously overweight. One can be overweight and still be starved for nutrients.

A long time ago, I adopted this principle: "Do not take one pound into the new year." It took discipline, but if I hadn't practiced this principle for thirty years, I might be thirty pounds heavier than I am today.

I emphasize diet in this discussion because it's a part of life that demands a lot of our attention. Eating is at the center of so many of our holidays, celebrations, and special events. Food was the method by which Satan tempted Adam and Eve in the garden of Eden. One of the greatest temptations the devil employs in his efforts to destroy mankind is the temptation of the appetite. The Bible tells us that when someone falls from temptation into sin, *"he is drawn away by his own desires and enticed"*

(James 1:14). The serpent beguiled Adam and Eve to appease the desires of their appetites and partake of food they knew was not intended for them, and the result was spiritual death.

When the serpent tempted Eve, she responded by explaining that God had commanded her and Adam not to eat of the tree *"in the midst of the garden...lest you die"* (Genesis 3:3). But the serpent was crafty in his counterattack.

> *The serpent said to the woman, "You will not surely die. For God knows that in the day you eat of it your eyes will be opened, and you will be like God, knowing good and evil." So when the woman saw that the tree was good for food, that it was pleasant to the eyes, and a tree desirable to make one wise, she took of its fruit and ate. She also gave to her husband with her, and he ate.* (Genesis 3:4–6)

Scripture records that the enemy appealed to Eve through her senses— sound, sight, and taste, in particular—and to her reason. He does the same thing to us, enticing us to eat when we aren't hungry by weakening our resistance to billboards plastered with pictures of tantalizing foods, TV advertisements for restaurants, and other appeals to eat.

Today, Satan still uses food to destroy mankind though even more crafty approaches. The Word of God says that *"people are destroyed for lack of knowledge"* (Hosea 4:6). Don't be ignorant of the enemy's devices. He uses eating disorders, poor nutrition, and lack of physical activity as keys to open the door to sickness and disease, which destroy our health. He tries to entice us by our own lusts and persuade us to overindulge.

God *"gives us richly all things to enjoy"* (1 Timothy 6:17), but not in excess. Proverbs 25:16 says, *"Have you found honey? Eat only as much as you need, lest you be filled with it and vomit."* We must train our bodies to eat for living, not to live for eating. There is absolutely nothing wrong with eating; however, gorging and excess are the arsenals that fuel our demise. As Proverbs 23:21 points out, *"The drunkard and the glutton will come to poverty, and drowsiness will clothe a man with rags."*

We must train our bodies to eat for living, not to live for eating.

It's not the will of God for you to be overtaken by the temptation to overeat. Just as with every temptation, He has promised to make a way of escape. We have this assurance in 1 Corinthians 10:13:

> No temptation has overtaken you except such as is common to man; but God is faithful, who will not allow you to be tempted beyond what you are able, but with the temptation will also make the way of escape, that you may be able to bear it.

Understand this: You have the power to overcome. Don't ever fall prey to the mind-set that food or anything else in life has power over you. God made you an overcomer, and you can win the battle against the enemy in all areas, including the area of food. Overeating, undereating, or abstaining from food altogether—it's all covered in the plan of victory through Jesus Christ. Don't give up, but stand your ground! *"Now thanks be to God who always leads us in triumph in Christ, and through us diffuses the fragrance of His knowledge in every place"* (2 Corinthians 2:14).

Balance Is Key

The enemy will use anything he can to cause us to defeat ourselves: overeating or starving ourselves, sleeping too much or being sleep deprived, or talking too much or rarely talking at all. If we surrender our wills to his persuasion, we allow him to take us from one extreme to the next. His goal is to sidetrack us on our pursuit of God's purpose, and so he manipulates everyday activities, like eating, sleeping, and talking, to beguile us. He will use anything, including things that our bodies require, such as food and rest, as weapons against us.

Anything in excess is too much and may affect our mental, emotional, and physical health and stability.

We require food to nourish us, sleep to restore us, and communication to express ourselves and interact with others. But when we practice these necessary things under the influence of the enemy, they can be used by him to perpetuate strongholds in our lives. Anything in excess is too much and may affect our mental, emotional, and physical health and stability. We need balance in every area of our lives.

I find that the healthier the food I consume, the more energy I have, and the less sleep I need. My need for rest is satisfied when I pay attention to what I eat. I think more clearly when my body is not loaded with fattening foods and sugary drinks. Indulging in heavy, hearty meals tends to weigh me down and make me want to lie down. What a waste of time! Eating a balanced diet of foods that provide proper nourishment gives the energy needed to be productive. When our diets are wholesome and nutrient-rich, they fuel our lives.

A well-balanced diet and regular physical activity are essential to good health. Many of the major health problems worldwide are due to poor nutritional choices and a lack of regular physical activity. Most diseases are preventable or treatable, as long as we make concerted efforts to adopt healthy lifestyles through proper diet and fitness. I'm suggesting that you adopt a lifestyle, not a short-lived diet. A lasting lifestyle change is essential to produce results that endure.

Eating Right

I am not a licensed nutritionist, but I do have a lifetime of experiences that can attest to the fact that eating right and exercising regularly will help to preserve and prolong your life. God's will with regard to our physical health—the wellness of our bodies—is the same as His will for our souls, as expressed by John in 3 John 1:2: *"Beloved, I pray that you may prosper in all things and be in health, just as your soul prospers."*

Our spirits are connected to our physical bodies, and we can monitor how well we are nourishing our spirits by paying attention to our natural bodies. Being deprived of adequate nutrients may cause malnutrition, fatigue, loss of muscle mass and tone, heart disease, brittle bones, diabetes, and many other conditions. But our bodies are designed with the capability of being rejuvenated.

For rejuvenation, the body needs a variety of vitamins and minerals, which carry disease-fighting compounds and powerful antioxidants. Eating right generates physical and mental energy to help you focus and be alert.

> *Eating right generates physical and mental energy to help you focus and be alert.*

Food Groups

There are three groups of nutrients that the body needs for optimal balance:

♦ **Carbohydrates:** A general term for a wide range of vegetables, fruits, cereals, and grains, which are excellent sources of energy. There are two types of carbohydrates: simple and complex. Simple carbohydrates are digested quickly, since they contain refined sugars and provide few necessary vitamins and minerals. Simple carbohydrates include fruits, vegetables, fruit juices, sodas, syrups, and jellies.

Complex carbohydrates, on the other hand, offer plenty of fiber, vitamins, and minerals. These can be found in starchy vegetables, multigrain breads, cereals, legumes, and pasta.

♦ **Protein:** Found in meat, fish, and dairy, as well as in plant foods, such as beans and lentils. Protein is essential to build, maintain, and repair body tissue.

♦ **Fat:** Found in meat, dairy products, nuts, seeds, and oils. It is essential for energy and for hormone production.

Plan daily to eat a balanced diet for health and vitality and shun foods that tend to weigh you down and produce unwanted pounds. Additionally, symptoms of sleepiness after eating suggest improper nutrient consumption.

After you have established a pattern of healthy eating, it will be easier for you to exercise on a regular basis. Exercise is a key component to being healthy. I could suggest a lot of things that may be beneficial, but consult with a physician to receive an exercise regimen that best fits your particular health needs.

You may be amazed to find out how much food you're consuming. Consider keeping a journal that records what you eat at every meal. Use your journal to help regulate your eating habits. It's really about discipline. Remember, eat three to five small meals a day rather than one or two large ones, for this will keep up your metabolism. To reduce the portion size of your meals, serve yourself on a salad plate rather than a dinner plate if it makes the portions seem larger to you. It's fine for you to eat that cheesecake—really, go ahead!—but stop when you're satisfied (which will probably happen before you've finished even one piece).

Above all, ask God to help you. He doesn't want you to be overweight or underweight; He wants you to be balanced and healthy. Give your diet to Him and ask for His help to regulate your eating habits and meal choices. The older we get, the slower our metabolisms become—unless we speed them up with vigorous exercise and foods high in protein, which boost the metabolic rate. You can't eat everything that you enjoyed in your youth. And if you're still a young woman, it's never too early to develop a healthy diet that will preserve and prolong your life.

> *It's fine for you to eat that cheesecake—but stop when you're satisfied.*

7

TEMPLE-BUILDING

Many people are unhealthy and out of shape merely because they lack the knowledge or know-how to regulate their bodies to burn fat. One of the most effective ways to lose weight and get in shape is not in a bottle nor available in stores. Exercise, which encompasses a wide variety of activities, when coupled with a balanced diet, will help you to lose weight and maintain a healthy heart. Adopting a regular regimen of cardiovascular exercise will increase your energy, regulate your heart rate, and help you to maintain or lose weight based on the intensity of your workout. Weight training and stretching are types of calisthenics you may want to incorporate in your daily routine.

For many of us, exercise is often no more than a notion. We have gone without it for so long that integrating it into our lifestyle seems difficult. But the reality is that when we exercise, we are adding years to our lives, so it must be included.

Dismiss the myth of believing you have to purchase a gym membership or a piece of expensive exercise equipment. Walking, gardening, shoveling snow, taking the stairs, and parking at a distance from the entrance to the mall or movie theater are all ways in which to invest in exercise. While watching television, you can stretch while sitting on the couch or hold on to the arm of the couch and do squats, which are excellent for improving circulation and building muscle. Find a partner to work out with who will hold you accountable to exercising regularly and remaining committed to a diligent regimen. Once exercise becomes routine, it will be easier and easier to do.

There are numerous methods of exercise that will help to increase your metabolism, range of motion, and stability, but there are two components of exercise that I encourage you to take part in daily because of their built-in benefits—stretching and breathing from the diaphragm.

Strength in Stretching

Stretching will increase your flexibility, help to prevent injury, and provide a faster recovery after completion of an exercise routine while it speeds removal of waste and toxins from your body and provides nutrients to your muscles. It also helps you to retain calcium and may aid in the prevention of osteoporosis. Studies have shown that after your muscles have been stretched, they recruit more fibers, giving you the flexibility to perform various tasks.

Other benefits of stretching include:

+ Stress relief
+ Increased body awareness and flexibility
+ Enhanced concentration
+ Improved circulation of blood and fluids to vital organs and tissues
+ Relief of muscle tension and stiffness
+ Increased levels of energy and stamina
+ Boosted immune system

Consult your physician or a fitness instructor about what types of exercise are best for you.

If you are new to regular exercise, it's time for you to begin a regimen that will assist you in increasing the longevity and quality of your life. The first thing I encourage you to do is consult your physician or a fitness instructor about what types of exercise are best for you. If your physician gives you the go-ahead, begin to incorporate exercise into your daily life by stretching every day. Stretching will get your body prepared for the other exercises that you will include later as you build your stamina and increase your strength.

Deep Breathing: Essential to Good Health

Slow, deep breathing is a powerful antistress technique. When you bring air down into the lower portion of the lungs, where the oxygen exchange is most efficient, heart rate slows, blood pressure decreases, muscles relax, anxiety eases, and the mind calms. Shallow "chest breathing" does not bring this kind of relief. All of our bodily actions—talking, singing, running, walking, talking, dancing, kicking, laughing, and so forth—require breathing. So why not breathe correctly?

Studies suggest that proper breathing technique is linked to ancient yoga and other meditation practices. However, if you were to hold a newborn baby, you would see that she breathes from her belly because that's the way God created us—to breathe from our diaphragms.

What kind of breather are you—a chest breather or a belly breather? To find out, try this test: place one hand on your chest and the other on your abdomen. Take a normal breath while looking down. If the hand on your chest rises first, you tend to breathe from your chest. If the hand on your abdomen rises first, you are more of a belly breather.

Studies have shown that few people in the Western world know how to breathe correctly. We are taught to stick out our chests and suck in our bellies; however, doing so will cause the muscles to become tense and will increase your respiration rate. Again, babies breathe from the belly, but with age, most people shift from this healthy abdominal breathing to shallow chest breathing.

> *With age, most people shift from healthy abdominal breathing to shallow chest breathing.*

Breathing is the only bodily function you can do either consciously or unconsciously. Focused breathing will help to reduce hot flashes in menopausal women, relieving chronic pain, and reducing symptoms of PMS. Some hospitals have begun teaching relaxation breathing to patients treated for a wide range of conditions. Diaphragmatic deep breathing is an essential practice of those training to be athletes, vocalists, public speakers, and dancers, among other professions.

I can't imagine that any "professional breathers" exist, but if there is such a profession, my husband deserves an honorary certification. He has been practicing breathing correctly for years. Years ago, he regularly trained the choir at our church to incorporate deep, diaphragmatic breathing when singing. He maintains that doing so produces a better vocal quality and sound, as well as provides the ability to hold a note longer or sing at a higher octave.

Deep Breathing through Meditation

In Joshua 1:8, God gave Joshua a powerful tool that is still available to us today: meditation. God instructed Joshua to keep the Word before his eyes and in his mouth and to meditate day and night. Although practiced in many cultures of the world, meditation originated in the Word of God and is one of the primary ways we can build our faith, stay conscious of God's presence, and even eliminate stress. The word *meditate* comes from the Hebrew word meaning "mutter"—speaking something to yourself over and over again.

> *Through meditation, we rehearse in our memories and speech the promises, precepts, and blessings God has declared to us in His Word.*

Through meditation, we rehearse in our memories and speech the promises, precepts, and blessings God has declared to us in His Word. It's more than sitting in silence and connecting with the atmosphere around you. Meditation makes the Word of God active in our thoughts; because it is alive and powerful and when we meditate, it brings us life. Constantly speaking the Word of God causes the Word to be planted deep in your heart, where it can take root and then produce a harvest in your life.

Below are a few prayers and corresponding Scriptures that you can use to meditate upon every day. Articulate them and allow them to transform your mind and increase your faith.

Father, give me the strength to do all that is written in Your Word. May I never turn aside from Your Word, give me Your courage in all that I do. Strengthen me and allow me to be bold in my walk with You.

(See Joshua 23:6; 1:8.)

Lord, perfect my life, not as I desire, but according to Your Word. You are the one who works in my life to do Your good pleasure; complete the good work You have begun in my life until the day of Christ.

(See Psalm 138:8; Philippians 4:13, 1:6.)

You, dear Father, are the Potter; and I am clay in Your hands. I am Your workmanship in Christ Jesus, created for good works. You have ordained my life. I was fashioned and formed to do Your works and those of Your kingdom.

(See Jeremiah 18:6; Ephesians 2:10.)

Make me a vessel of honor, sanctified and useful for Your use. Thank You for making me a woman of God, complete and equipped for every good work. As a servant of Christ, I labor fervently in prayer that I *"may stand perfect and complete in all the will of God."*

(See 2 Timothy 2:21, 3:17; Colossians 4:12.)

Perfect my heart in You, Lord, as I walk in Your statues and keep Your commandments. Give me the help I need to behave myself wisely. I declare that I will not look at the things that are behind me but look ahead and press toward the mark for the prize of the high calling of God, which is in Christ Jesus, our Lord.

(See Ezekiel 20:19; Psalm 101:2; Philippians 3:12–14.)

Thank You that I was buried with Christ by baptism into His death and, like Christ, was raised from the dead by Your glory. I pray I walk in newness of life. As I walk after the Spirit and not my flesh. I pray to remember there is now no condemnation for those in Christ Jesus because You have made me free from the law of sin and death.

(See Romans 6:4, 8:1–2.)

Don't be afraid to exercise and never become too busy to make it a part of your daily life. Once again, consult with your physician about what exercises may be right for you and get on the road to longevity. Though it may take some effort to become engaged in regular exercise initially, when you adapt it into your lifestyle and do it properly you will feel invigorated and less likely to consume that piece of apple pie when you're done and experience two feelings of accomplishment; the discipline to exercise and the ability not to give in to the appetites of your flesh.

8

REST AND RELAXATION

Hebrews 4:9 talks about a supernatural rest that belongs to the people of God: *"There remains therefore a rest for the people of God."* The word for *"rest"* used in this passage comes from the Greek word *sabbatismos,* from which we get the English word *Sabbath.* It means "the blessed rest from toils and troubles."

As women of God, we should partake of that type of rest, allowing it to minister to every facet of who we are. The rest that God has for us is free from toil and troubles because it is based on total trust in Him.

Taking time to rest is an act of wisdom. It affords you the opportunity of investing in yourself. Rest and relaxation belong to you. They lead to a state of physical, spiritual, and mental peace; it's not merely a good night's sleep.

Rest begins inwardly and works its way out when you allow God, through the Holy Spirit, to free your overworked mind or troubled heart. It is living in a divine place inherited from God, promised and set aside just for you.

Thus the heavens and the earth, and all the host of them, were finished. And on the seventh day God ended His work which He had done, and He rested on the seventh day from all His work which He had done.

(Genesis 2:1–2)

We have to put things in perspective and understand that we have only twenty-four hours in every day. God Himself took His time creating the heavens and the earth. If anyone had the capacity to do it all in one day, it would be God, but He wasn't in a hurry.

He is our example. He took His time, so you and I can be free of the mentality that we have to do it all in a day. If we prioritize our time and put God first, He will give us the wisdom necessary to accomplish what we need to each day.

When you are constantly rushing around and running against the clock, you will never feel like you have accomplished anything. Instead, you will feel a perpetual sense of defeat.

Beloved Sleep

It is vain for you to rise up early, to sit up late, to eat the bread of sorrows; for so He gives His beloved sleep. (Psalm 127:2)

Sleep is essential for good health, mental and emotional functioning, and safety. God has given it to us to revive our bodies and minds. The Bible says that it's vanity to get up early and stay up late, which suggests that we are out of balance when we do so. How can our bodies, souls, and spirits be balanced when we burn the candlewick at both ends? Researchers have found that individuals with poor sleep habits are more likely than others to develop several kinds of psychiatric problems and are also likely to make greater use of health care services.

> *Most women need an average of seven to eight hours of sleep per night.*

Even occasional sleeping problems can make daily life feel more stressful or cause you to be less productive. A lack of sleep will produce difficulty concentrating, accomplishing required tasks, and handling minor irritations. Along these lines, my husband once preached a sermon entitled "The Devil Loves Tired People." Tired people make poor decisions that they would not ordinarily make if they've received adequate rest.

Sleep needs vary from person to person. In general, most women need an average of seven to eight hours of sleep per night. However, some individuals can function without being sleepy or drowsy after only six. Others cannot perform at their peak unless they have slept ten hours.

In order to get a good night's sleep, here are a few tips that may be helpful to you:

- Avoid food and beverages containing caffeine later in the day, as they can inhibit your ability to settle down and fall asleep.

- If you have trouble sleeping when you go to bed, don't nap during the day.

- Exercise regularly, but do so at least three hours prior to bedtime. A workout after that time can keep you awake because your body has not had the chance to cool itself down.

- Establish a regular, relaxing bedtime routine that will allow you to unwind and send a signal to your brain that it is time to sleep.

- Avoid exposure to bright lights before bedtime.

- Taking a hot bath may also help.

- Make your sleeping environment pleasant, comfortable, dark, and as quiet as possible.

Take the time to relax and allow yourself the privilege of falling into a deep, tranquil sleep.

9

THE OIL OF ESTHER:
PREPARING TO MEET THE KING

"Let the king appoint officers in all the provinces of his kingdom, that they may gather all the beautiful young virgins to Shushan the citadel, into the women's quarters, under the custody of Hegai the king's eunuch, custodian of the women. And let beauty preparations be given them. Then let the young woman who pleases the king be queen instead of Vashti." This thing pleased the king, and he did so.

(Esther 2:3–4)

The story of Esther is a powerful message of God's delivering power to an entire nation of people because of the boldness of one young woman. Esther was special. Her name means "star," and, like a star, she was revered by her people for two reasons: she delivered them from death, and she was chosen as the bride of King Ahasuerus.

When Esther was preparing to marry the king, she wasn't merely preparing for her wedding day; she was getting ready for *life*. (See Esther 2:1–18.) It was the custom in that day for a woman to be lavishly pampered for an entire year prior to marrying a king.

Day after day, Esther underwent necessary physical preparations in order to prepare her body for the king. From cleansing and purifying to fasting and praying, Esther was being transformed through what equated to an "extreme makeover." Esther was beautiful, but she was also modest and unaccustomed to the lavish care that she received from her seven maidservants. She was an orphan, but God was preparing her for royalty, ministry, and greatness.

For six months, her body was cleansed in myrrh, which is often used in aromatherapy because of its purifying, healing, and elevating characteristics. In this particular case, myrrh represented death to the flesh (Esther's old way of doing things).

> *Esther positioned herself to receive blessings, and because she did not skip any part of the long preparatory process, she became a queen.*

For another six months after this, Esther was pampered in fragrant oils and cosmetics. Speaking from a life perspective, Esther positioned herself to receive blessings, and because she did not skip any part of the long preparatory process, she became a queen. Preparation is not lost time. Like He did with Esther, God is positioning you for greatness, but you don't want to forgo the preparatory process. Those who fail to prepare themselves risk being like the five foolish virgins in the parable of the wise and foolish virgins, who were not prepared when the bridegroom came. (See Matthew 25:1–13.)

It is necessary to put in order each facet of the fabric of your life. Take care of your body and make yourself ready for the return of our King; He wants your spirit poised, your mind polished, and your body well-postured. Come to understand your worth, and know that you represent God on the earth. You're a part of a royal priesthood (see 1 Peter 2:9); you, too, are a queen who needs to make time to invest in the care of herself on a regular basis. You never know where you'll be summoned as God's representative on any given day.

Esther is an excellent example of how a woman's body can be purified and pampered. Like Esther, we want the pleasure of treating our own bodies in this most luxurious way.

God has given us all that is needed to keep our bodies alive, and we must learn to be the best caretakers we can possibly be. I am going to provide practical guidelines for caring for several of the various components God has given us that make up the body and that we often neglect, beginning with the most visible: our skin.

Loving the Skin You're In

The skin is the largest organ of the body. It is elastic, flexible tissue that has a divine purpose from God. Our skin is not merely wrapping paper holding our bones and muscles together; it is a living, changing mantle. Whatever is happening in our spiritual or natural lives, positive or negative, is often reflected in our skin. Simple phrases like "You're glowing," or "You look flushed" remind us that we can rarely hide our inner selves. Besides mirroring our feelings, our skin speaks silently as it changes and reveals who we are.

> *Whatever is happening in our spiritual or natural lives, positive or negative, is often reflected in our skin.*

Daily Skincare Treatments

Maintain a good cleansing regimen inclusive of facial cleansers (cream or liquid), gentle scrubs, eye makeup remover, toner (astringent), eye cream, masks, and a high-quality moisturizer is important. Cleansing and treating your facial skin morning and evening will produce vibrant, even tone facial skin.

Hydrating the Skin

Immersing in and drinking water makes the body more relaxed and invigorated. It also replaces the moisture lost due to everyday activities. Water primarily stimulates the circulation of blood, fluids, and other elements inside our bodies. Additionally, water regulates and brings natural balance to the skin. Warm water has the power to hydrate, revitalize, detoxify, and oxygenate the skin. Warm water also gets rid of blackheads and reduces the size of pores. Our skin becomes dry and dehydrated when we have not consumed an adequate amount of water, so one of the easiest and most effective ways to rejuvenate our bodies is by drinking enough of this vital fluid on a daily basis. It is absolutely essential for maintaining the mineral balance that keeps our cells working well and enables our bodies to function optimally. The ideal amount of water consumption per day is half of your body weight in ounces. For example, if you weigh 160 pounds, you should drink 80 ounces of water each day, or eight glasses. I recommend filling a 64-ounce bottle with water, preferably room temperature, and refilling it at least once. Carrying the bottle with you, keeping it at work or where you spend the most time during the day, will help you consume your necessary water intake daily. So don't forget your water bottle!

Creating Your Own Home Spa

> *You can create a spa experience at home that will be available the instant the need arises or time permits.*

Can't get to a spa as often as you'd like? You can create a spa experience at home that will be available the instant the need arises or time permits. Here are some ideas to help you pamper, relax, and rejuvenate right at home. To create your own home spa experience, set aside one to two hours when you will not be interrupted. If this isn't possible, don't dismiss the idea altogether. Claim whatever time is available to you and use it wisely!

Keep your bathroom clean and clutter-free so that it's a pleasant, safe place to rest. It doesn't have to be a large space to be special; you can transform any bathroom into a home spa.

Before we continue, I have a few notes of caution. When using oils, be sure to use area rugs to prevent slipping. Place candles in a clutter-free area to avoid creating a fire hazard. Additionally, keep all electrical appliances away from water.

Now you are ready for a peaceful spa.

Make sure that your bathroom is clean and fresh. To create a soothing environment, start by evoking a relaxing atmosphere in your bathing area with soft lighting, scented candles, and soothing music. An inflatable bath pillow makes lounging in the bath more comfortable.

Light your favorite aromatherapy candles. Aromatherapy scents can relax or revive.

You may stimulate the auditory senses by playing soothing music or recordings of nature sounds that relax and inspire. The sound of a water fountain is just perfect for evoking a relaxing mood. Or, perhaps it is silence that you crave.

Spa Fitness

Start your special spa day with exercise—aerobics, walking, playing tennis, strength training, or whatever works for you.

Spa Cuisine

Treat yourself to a deliciously nutritious meal to celebrate at day's end. Healthy food makes you feel great, gives you energy, and boosts your metabolism. If you are what you eat, do you really want to resemble a double bacon cheeseburger with the works and a side of greasy fries? Treat yourself to a nutritionally balanced spa dish at least once each week. Make time. You deserve it!

Spa Treatments

Though we may not always have time for application, every woman wants soft skin and a healthy glow. Body treatments and oils can be instrumental in helping us achieve this simple luxury. Additionally, body scrubs and exfoliants like Dead Sea salts and sugars mixed with oils are useful in removing dead skin. These are practices we can incorporate on a regular basis. Instead of taking a shower seven days a week, consider making time to bathe at least two of those days. With our busy schedules, we seldom have time to bathe, so we must *put it* on our calendars.

Treat yourself to a nutritionally balanced spa dish at least once each week.

By making time to revitalize your skin, you will add to your skin's nourishment. There is a wide variety of skin-care products on the market today, and they range in price. Finding one that meets your particular budget and skin-care needs can be easy.

Facial Masks

Take care to remove any makeup, unwanted body hairs, fingernail polish, and so forth beforehand. Then, apply a facial mask. Dry-brush entire body to exfoliate or rub on a salt scrub made from equal parts salt and canola oil.

Body Wraps

When you plan a spa visit, think about trying a body wrap. This treatment hydrates your skin and softens it through a combination of moisturized wrappings composed of oil-soaked sheets and heated blankets. You would do well to set aside some time and resources to fully partake of this opulent experience. Another exquisite moisturizing technique you may enjoy is the mud bath, in which the earth's own nutrients are used to enrich your skin.

Stress Relief

Everyone experiences stress. When we are overwhelmed by stress, it can affect our health. That's why effective stress relievers are essential in restoring our physical health. Following is a list of activities that can help alleviate stress in your life; however, one woman's effective form of stress relief may not be another's.

+ Sing fun, upbeat, uplifting songs (singing with family members or friends adds even more fun).

+ Visit an aquarium, zoo, or museum.

+ Pump up the volume (try *Darrell Hines Live*) and start housecleaning.

+ Take a Pilates class.

+ Relieve yourself of unnecessary obligations.

+ Play a game with friends.

+ Walk the dog.

+ Doodle or draw a picture.

+ Fly a kite.

+ Take a mini-vacation.

+ Put on your dancing shoes.

+ Keep a journal.

+ Watch an old movie—classic, comedy, Western, you name it.

+ Shovel snow.

+ Plant flowers; tend a garden.

+ Ride a bike.

+ Take a hike.

+ Read a good book (like the one you're reading!).

This is by no means an exhaustive list, but it offers a few simple ideas that you may or may not have considered to help relieve stress. And after you've relieved stress actively, there's no better thing to do than delight yourself in a relaxing bath.

The Soothing Bath

A soothing, relaxing bath is a great means to relieve stress; mixing the proper oils and integrating the right fragrances will minister relaxation and healing. As stated in Proverbs 27:9, *"Ointment and perfume delight the heart."*

Did you realize that you can use some everyday household products and pantry staples for spa treatments? That you can bathe in the same ingredient you use to dress your salad—olive oil? Soak in the same thing that complements your breakfast cereal—milk? Can you envision scrubbing your skin with the same seasonings that wake up your taste buds—sugar and salt?

When I think about all the things that were made for human consumption that we can also use for moisturizing and soothing our bodies, it amazes me. Almonds and honey for the skin, mayonnaise for the hair and cucumbers for the eyes are only a few of many foods that we don't have to consume in order for them to bring pleasure to our bodies. We can take

> *We can take pleasure bathing, showering, and moisturizing with the same foods that we take pleasure in eating.*

pleasure bathing, showering, and moisturizing with the same foods that we take pleasure in eating.

Adding natural oils and minerals to our baths can be therapeutic. For instance, chamomile leaves have soothing, healing properties that ease away tension. To fully enjoy the medicinal assets of the chamomile plant, brew three cups of very strong leaves and add the concentrate to your bathwater.

Mixing two teaspoons of ginger with two teaspoons of dried mustard and adding the mixture to your bath is an effective way to treat menstrual bloating and discomfort.

You can soothe your muscles by applying a thin film of bath oil over your shoulders and neck. Drape a large towel over your shoulders and step into the shower. The towel's wet, warm heat will help the oil penetrate your skin, softening it as it also relaxes your muscles. Essential oils added to your bath can relax your muscles, help you sleep, relieve pain, make you feel more alert, and help clear congestion in your sinuses and chest.

Along with essential oils, there are many other products you can use that will be soothing and therapeutic for your skin. For some items, you may need to make a trip to the store; for others, you don't have to look any further than your kitchen to find luxurious items for your bath.

Salt Bath

The ingredients for this treatment consist simply of Epsom salt, sea salt, and essential oils. While you're in the tub, sprinkle some of the oil and salt mixture on a sponge or cloth and use it to scrub your skin to remove dry, dead cells and to stimulate circulation. Epson salts are thought to speed the elimination of toxins from the body through the skin. Now I understand why my mother kept a box of Epson salt on the side of the tub. When you are through, thoroughly rinse the salt from your body.

Oatmeal Bath

For baby-soft skin, measure a cup of oatmeal into a double cheesecloth bag and swirl the bag around under the faucet while the water is running. Once you're in the tub, scrub your body with the bag. Your skin will feel wonderful afterward.

Olive Oil and Milk Bath

Blend half a cup of olive oil with one quart of whole milk or cream and add the mixture to a warm bath for a rich, relaxing soak.

Essential Oils

Pure plant essential oils have been used for thousands of years to relieve stress, promote restful sleep, clear the mind, and energize the body. There are nine basic aromatherapy oil blends: three to help you feel awake and energized, three for stress relief, and three to promote restful sleep.

If you're working late on a project and need to stay awake, try the following:

Grapefruit and peppermint	*known for its uplifting and reviving properties*
Orange and ginger	*invigorates the senses*
Bergamot and coriander	*boosts energy*

If you need to relax, try the following:

Eucalyptus and spearmint	*renowned for its calming powers*
Cedarwood and sage	*highly regarded for its soothing properties*
Blue lavender and palmarosa	*helps relieve stress*

If you've had a long day and need to sleep, try the following:

Lavender and vanilla	*promotes tranquility*
Sweet bay and rose	*promotes relaxation and clears the mind; an ideal companion to the calming rose essence from France*
Chamomile and Neroli	*widely used for its deeply relaxing and calming nature; Neroli contributes feelings of peace and harmony as it rejuvenates the skin*

Consider these oil blends when purchasing therapeutics and aromatherapy products for your home spa.

Hands and Fingers, Feet and Toes

> *Our hands and feet serve us diligently every day, yet we often overlook the rough treatment they receive.*

Your pampering isn't complete until you've beautified your hands and feet! Our hands and feet serve us diligently every day, yet we often overlook the rough treatment they receive. Our hands are exposed to pollutants, elements, and chemicals, and they're subjected to overuse, particularly by our constant use of computer keyboards, cell phone keypads, and various appliances and machinery.

Though our feet serve us faithfully, we tend to consider fashion over comfort when we shop for footwear, looking good at the expense of arch support and expecting them to bear our weight in tiny heels. Our hands and feet cry out in anguish in the form of calluses, dryness, and itchiness, screaming, "Take care of me, please!"

If your hands resemble crumpled leaves and your feet refuse to take you another step, then your appendages are overworked and in need of pampering. If you're able to give yourself a manicure or pedicure, that's great for maintenance, but I encourage and implore you to allow yourself to be pampered by a licensed professional. Alternatively, perhaps you and a friend can give each other hand and foot treatments. Whatever you choose, purpose to set aside time to receive hand and foot pampering.

Take a Hand

Thank God for hands. With them, you can hold the hand of the one you love, clean a house, paint a picture, or pen a prolific dissertation. Our hands are probably one of the most useful body parts we have, and we often neglect to give them proper care. Caring for our hands and fingers entails more than merely getting regular manicures.

Even so, keeping your nails groomed is an important finishing touch to your beauty routine. Give them regular attention, cleaning and trimming them daily and filing them weekly. If you wear polish, be sure to keep it fresh, removing it before it starts to peel. You may want to use a nail brush to clean debris that may be trapped under the nail.

Remember the slogan, "Milk...it does a body good"? Well, this is true, especially when it comes to your hands and nails. Soaking your hands in a warm cup of whole milk for five minutes will strengthen your hands and nails, as well as hydrate your skin.

Keep in mind the following guidelines for strong, smooth hands and nails:

1. Wear gloves whenever you use any kind of chemical or cleaning agent that could be harmful to praying hands.

2. Exfoliate and moisturize daily.

3. Avoid extremely hot water and harsh solvents.

4. Massage and flex your fingers, hands, and wrists daily.

5. Dry your hands thoroughly after washing them.

6. Add a teaspoon of almond oil to dishwater to seal moisture in hands when you're not wearing rubber gloves.

Make a Stand

The Word of God says, *"How beautiful are the feet of those who preach the gospel of peace"* (Romans 10:15). The American Orthopaedic Foot and Ankle Society reports that 90 percent of women wear shoes that are one to two sizes too small. For foot health, make sure you measure your feet properly and purchase comfortably fitting footwear with ample space for flexing your toes.

Are you aware that in your lifetime, you have the potential to walk a distance that's equivalent to the circumference of the world—times four? It's hard to imagine walking 115,000 miles, but that is the average distance a person covers from when she's a toddler to her golden years. Our feet really deserve pampering. So, make a stand to care for your feet regularly.

Keep your heels free of excessively dry and dead skin by moisturizing and exfoliating. Apply an emollient lotion regularly. Peppermint foot lotion keeps feet soft, fresh-smelling, and moisturized. Regular pedicures, whether professional or at home, help keep feet looking and feeling great. If you're planning to paint your toenails, make sure they are neatly polished, especially when you wear sandals.

Of all the clothing that we wear, we have only one garment that will be worn perpetually, and that is our skin. Daily care is essential to help our bodies endure years of wear. Remember, you have only one body, so make sure you add more to it than the apparel you don daily. Proper nutrients, natural remedies, and essential oils are necessary to the preservation of your body, so spend time getting to know your body and learn what brings healing and soundness to your flesh.

10

BODY: A LANGUAGE WITHOUT WORDS

You are our epistle written in our hearts, known and read by all men;
clearly you are an epistle of Christ, ministered by us, written not with
ink but by the Spirit of the living God, not on tablets of stone but on
tablets of flesh, that is, of the heart.
—2 Corinthians 3:2–3

Like an ornate tapestry depicting a storybook scene, you can speak volumes without uttering one word. Your nonverbal communication often drowns out what you say, and chances are, other people will remember what you did more than they will what you said. "Actions speak louder than words" is a popular saying, probably because it seems to ring true.

What we think—or say in our heads—about ourselves comes across to others in how we present ourselves. That's why we should purpose to present ourselves as living sacrifices, holy and acceptable to God. (See Romans 12:1.) Even before you speak, others will make judgments about you based on generalizations they draw from your appearance and actions. Has anyone ever told you that he or she was initially disinclined to like you? Has a friend told you, "When I first met you, I didn't like you"? These are just a few examples of how people prejudge. Perhaps your appearance makes others inclined to assume they won't get along with you. What do your nonverbal communication and your body language convey to others about you? How is your Christian walk defined? As others carefully read the pages of your life, what do they see? What conclusions will they draw?

What else might we be saying when we...

+ **Smile?**
  "I feel good." _____ _____
+ **Make a gesture?**
  "Come here." _____ _____
+ **Nod our heads?**
  "Yes." _____ _____
+ **Slump in our chairs?**
  "I don't want to be here." _____ _____
+ **Stomp our feet?**
  "I'm mad!" _____ _____
+ **Smack our lips?**
  "Whatever!" _____ _____
+ **Laugh?**
  "That's funny." _____ _____
+ **Cry?**
  "I'm feeling overwhelmed." _____ _____
+ **Raise our eyebrows?**
  "Hmm." _____ _____
+ **Roll our eyes?**
  "Here we go again." _____ _____

I Can Hear What You're Saying with My Eyes

If you want to mask your feelings, pay close attention to your nonverbal behavior, for it may betray what your mouth will not.

Research in communication has suggested that only 7 to 35 percent of a message is conveyed through words, while the remaining portion—the majority—is conveyed through nonverbal expressions. The power of nonverbal communication is often underestimated, but nonverbal communication cues you in to what another person is thinking or feeling, based on his or her facial expressions, gestures, comportment, and so forth.

Nonverbal communication includes everything from tone of voice to posture, from signs to use of space. Different cultures ascribe various meanings to certain looks, gestures, and other nonverbal cues.

If you want to mask your feelings, pay close attention to your nonverbal behavior, for it may betray what your mouth will not. If you are about to give someone difficult news—announcing the death of a loved one to a family member, for instance—your voice and diction may be under control, but your nonverbal body language, including the tiniest facial expression or minutest movement, may give away the news before you can speak it.

When you enter a room, does your appearance command attention, or do you walk in unnoticed? When your composure is intact and you are well-groomed, graceful, and poised, your presence may command unspoken attention. If you walk in the same room wearing inappropriate attire, you may attract unwanted attention. What "air" are you releasing when you're in the company of others?

Your outward appearance conveys a great deal about you. The ways you walk, stand, sit, and maintain your posture communicate your personal attributes to others. If you have confidence and grace, it will be evident in your poise. At all times, you want to try to put your best foot forward. You want your posture to communicate positive truths about your character. Poise is the proper behavior by which a woman conducts herself. A poised woman displays dignity, good posture, and refinement in her stance, stride, and manner.

> *A poised woman displays dignity, good posture, and refinement in her stance, stride, and manner.*

As a godly woman, you are to be a living epistle, known and read by everyone. So, you have to be careful of the message you are transmitting when you communicate with your body.

Chastity—A Rare Virtue

The book of Proverbs includes a list of attributes that characterize a "*virtuous woman*" (Proverbs 31:10 KJV). When the Bible describes the virtuous woman, it delves into the details of her life: her children bless her, she is a shrewd businesswoman and merchant, she possesses strength and honor, she manages her household with efficiency and wisdom, and her husband's heart can trust fully in her. (See Proverbs 31:11–28.) Her talents and skills are versatile; she doesn't have one specific virtue that defines her. Many are the things she does well.

There are women who can manage Fortune 500 companies, but can they manage their homes? A virtuous woman can do both. According to the description in Proverbs 31, she does many things well; like a beautiful diamond, she is multifaceted. She is a woman of distinction, honor, and chastity—an attribute we should all aspire to.

In the twenty-first century, the virtue of chastity has been largely overlooked and even dismissed by mainstream media because sexuality has come to govern most of what appeals to the natural man.

Most women want to appeal to men; they want to be sexy. But a chaste woman doesn't try to be noticed by society for her sexuality. She has sophisticated appeal independent of her sex appeal.

> *A chaste woman has sophisticated appeal independent of her sex appeal.*

Make no mistake: I am not suggesting that a curvaceous body implies that a woman can't be chaste, or even that a chaste woman can't be appealing. As a matter of fact, a woman of character, integrity, and chastity who is also attractive and physically fit is especially beautiful because of the way these attributes complement one another.

When a woman reclaims her appeal to practice chastity, she is less likely to attract lewd men. A virtuous woman will not live in sexual immorality. (See 1 John 3:6 AMP.) When she has the nature of God in her, she doesn't have to appeal to men's desires. She's chaste in her conversation, her walk, her dress, and how she interacts with men.

A chaste woman's beauty is admired in appropriate ways. She is respected and esteemed. Consider yourself esteemed if a brother respectfully offers to hold the door, pulls out your chair, smiles kindly, or extends some other form of courtesy. Don't assume that he's trying to hit on you; rather, reply with a smile, a pleasant expression of gratitude, or a few moments of small talk. (And by "small talk," I don't mean, "Here's my number and a dime; call me anytime.")

A virtuous woman lets him move first. When you're the first, you may lose his respect, even if it doesn't show immediately. If he doesn't have the courage to ask you for your number, or if he doesn't seem interested in taking your relationship to the next level, don't try to do it anyway! Stay in control of yourself and your emotions. A true gentleman never forces his will on a lady, and the standards are no different for the lady. Every lady is a woman, but not every woman is a lady, for a lady is *always* chaste. Some women think being chaste is boring and unattractive. Queen Esther was one of the most beautiful women to ever live, but I believe she possessed a quality that elated King Ahasuerus. And this is maybe why he chose her to be the queen over thousands of others.

Investing in Your Soul

INVESTING IN YOUR SOUL

L ong before makeover shows became popular, I hosted a citywide "Image Is Everything" seminar at a local hotel. It was well-attended. We invited professionals from various facets of the fashion industry to serve as consultants and offer beauty tips to the women who were participating. Among the numerous door prizes was the grand prize, which included a free makeover. What's wonderful is that the woman who won was in great need of a makeover. She was the mother of three children, the youngest a newborn, the oldest a toddler, and the cares of being a wife and mother had bombarded her to the point that she regularly forsook her own care.

Our resident beauty consultants, makeup artists, and hairstylists took our special guest and exchanged her dungarees and pigtails for a becoming ensemble and a new coiffure. The colors in her clothing accentuated the beauty of her perfectly applied foundation, mascara, eye shadow, and blush. She looked absolutely radiant and totally transformed. The audience was so stunned by her transformation that they gave a standing ovation for her and her stylists. Everyone was elated, especially our model, who was overjoyed to the point of tears.

The next day was Sunday. As we assembled for the morning's service and I looked out at the congregation, I couldn't help but notice our model walk in the back door with her children. When I beheld her, I was completely flabbergasted. Every one of her precisely spiraled curls had come unwound. The makeup we had sent home with her must have been left in the packaging—either that, or she had dismissed the application techniques the artists had explained to her. She made her way to her seat and sat there looking a lot like Cinderella after the magic had worn off.

This woman was dealing with great internal turmoil that made it difficult for her to maintain her makeover. Inwardly, she was scarred. The fabric of who she had become was tattered and torn. The emotional abuse she had suffered wore on her like a shroud. Though her outward appearance had been made over, she could not receive true transformation because the agony of her internal conflict was causing her to walk in defeat.

Her situation reminds me of a makeover show that was aired some years ago called *The Swan*. Before participating, each contestant first had to agree to receive professional counseling and therapy before undergoing a cosmetic makeover. The reason for this requirement was that each contestant had a low sense of self-worth; each considered herself to be an "ugly duckling." The creators and producers of the show were wise to realize the danger of beautifying the outside without paying close attention and care to the mind, as well.

Having a sound mind is essential to developing your total being. Be careful about the thoughts you keep, for your soul is where your emotions are lodged. That's why the apostle Paul entreated us to "[cast] *down arguments and every high thing that exalts itself against the knowledge of God, bringing every thought into captivity to the obedience of Christ*" (2 Corinthians 10:5). If a thought that enters your mind doesn't correspond with God's Word, don't process it. Instead, make it captive to the obedience of Christ. In other words, arrest every negative, contrary thought that comes to mind, annulling it with the Word of God.

Depression and mental illness never discriminate; rich and poor, black and white, and young and old alike are battling various forms of mental illness, which have taken root in the mind. That's why Jesus gave us these words of encouragement: "*Let not your heart be troubled; you believe in God, believe also in Me*" (John 14:1). What you believe, how you think, and the way you process your thoughts will determine whether your mind is sound. A sound mind is a gift from God to you. It needs to be cultivated and renewed daily. When you exchange your thoughts for His, you can receive healing and restoration, and your mind will be sound.

I have had the privilege of meeting women from many cultural, socio-economic, and racial backgrounds, and there is a common thread found in the majority; we want to look our very best. When a woman wears beautiful clothes, it makes her feel good, and we emphasize looking good. As we sport stunning hairstyles, fine jewelry, and fashionable clothes, let's also exhibit inner beauty by dressing in godly character. Don't allow your outer adornment to take precedence over beautifying the inner. Whether wearing Adidas or Armani, let's become conscious of allowing our beauty to radiate from within, because our beauty should first be an expression of who we are in Christ.

I believe that God wants us to wear the absolute finest, but I also believe He wants us to find balance dressing our bodies, feeding our minds, and developing our spirits. As an ambassador for Christ (see 2 Corinthians 5:20), you should always look your best, inside and out.

While we are called by God to be ambassadors, God's primary interest is the conditions of our hearts. God desires our primary investment to be from the inside out. So, let's invest in our souls, develop spiritual maturity, and learn to cultivate godly compassion, in addition to investing in our outward appearance.

When was the last time you invested in a good Bible or book, besides this one, that ministered to and helped you mature spiritually? If it's been a while, it's time to make that investment now. Invest in your soul and spirit by meditating on God's Word and entering into fellowship with Him. Make your number one priority being pleasing to God.

11

IT IS WELL WITH MY SOUL

T he soul is the seat of our emotions and decisions; it comprises our minds, wills, and emotions. The soul is a very complex component of our total beings. Mentioned more than 458 times in the Word of God, our souls can be lost, saved, vexed, happy, overwhelmed, restored, lifted up in vanity, converted, or dwelling at ease. But most important, our souls can be blessed.

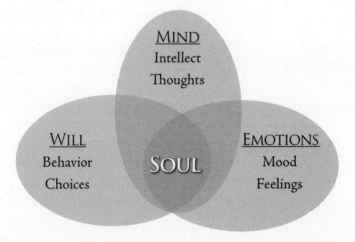

Our souls are an essential part of us, and if we can bring them into balance with our spirits, our bodies will follow. As stated above, the soul involves the mind, will, and intellect. This chapter will explore various aspects of the soul, how they work, and how to use God's Word to renew our minds, regulate our emotions, and bless our souls.

Bless the LORD, *O my soul; and all that is within me, bless His holy name! Bless the* LORD, *O my soul, and forget not all His benefits: Who forgives all your iniquities, Who heals all your diseases, Who redeems your life from destruction, Who crowns you with lovingkindness and tender mercies, Who satisfies your mouth with good things, so that your youth is renewed like the eagle's.* (Psalm 103:1–5)

Anchored in the Lord

In those times when your soul becomes weary and overwhelmed, if you are anchored in the Lord, you can be assured that He will restore your soul. David experienced many such occurrences, which he recorded throughout the Psalms. Because he had a personal relationship with God, David's soul had a place in Him.

The LORD *is my shepherd; I shall not want. He makes me to lie down in green pastures; He leads me beside the still waters. He **restores my soul**; He leads me in the paths of righteousness for His name's sake.* (Psalm 23:1–3, emphasis added)

Women have to endure a lot. Our minds are overloaded with the constant challenges we face that seek to rob us of one of life's simplest yet most rewarding pleasures: peace of mind. From the corporate CEO who works long hours and sometimes loses herself in her work to the single mother of five who is consumed with the countless activities, practices, and performances that crowd her schedule, women need to make time for themselves and take breaks from the demands on their lives. Even if you're able to do it all, neglecting your soul will prove highly detrimental. Matthew 16:26 asks, "*What profit is it to a man if he gains the whole world, and loses his own soul? Or what will a man give in exchange for his soul?*"

> *The key to enjoying peace of mind is simply trusting God.*

The key to enjoying peace of mind is simply trusting God. Say with the psalmist, "*I will say of the Lord, He is my Refuge and my Fortress, my God; on Him I lean and rely, and in Him I [confidently] trust!*" (Psalm 91:2 AMP). If you will learn to trust God and take

Him at His word, the empty and broken places of your life will be made whole, and you will have peace of mind.

When we fail to take God at His word and instead doubt His promises, we miss the opportunity to be what He has purposed us to be. God has already made available to us all things that pertain to life and godliness (see 2 Peter 1:3), but if we stand on the perimeters of His presence and fail to enter into its fullness, we will miss His purposes for our lives and lose our sense of peace.

If you are not acquainted with Him through continual fellowship, how can you know the things that He has made freely available to you? You need to develop a relationship with God—a real one with increasing depth. When you have fellowship with God, then your confidence is built so that when you ask Him anything, you know He will grant your petitions. First John 5:14–15 says, *"Now this is the confidence that we have in Him, that if we ask anything according to His will, He hears us. And if we know that He hears us, whatever we ask, we know that we have the petitions that we have asked of Him."* That's how I live my life. As a matter of fact, that is the Scripture on which the church my husband and I pastor was founded!

When you have allowed God's Word to transform you, then you will possess the ability to cast down *"imaginations"*—thoughts loaded with doubt, fear, and unbelief. (See 2 Corinthians 10:5 KJV.) Doubt, fear, and unbelief are tormenting spirits, and God has not given them to you. He's given you *power* over your thought life, His *love* to protect you, and *soundness of mind* to vanquish every thought that does not promote peace. (See 2 Timothy 1:7.)

Try not to spend too much time thinking about what will happen if things don't work out the way you think they should. Instead, spend more time meditating on what God's Word says about every situation. It is so much better to cast down *"imaginations"* than to dwell on them.

> *Spend more time meditating on what God's Word says about every situation.*

Once you put this into practice—casting off negative thoughts rather than letting them fester in your mind—it will become easier until it's a part of your nature. Dwelling on such questions as, "What will I do if I get laid off?" and "When will this pain ever go away?" invokes fear, and fear, as I stated before, is torment. The more you think about the situation, the more you give audience to the dictates of the enemy, or thief—Satan—who comes *"to steal, and to kill, and to destroy,"* but Jesus came that we *"may have life...more abundantly"* (John 10:10).

> *While the enemy attempts daily to steal, kill, and destroy us, Jesus' death, burial, and resurrection assure that we have life abundantly.*

Whereas the enemy endeavors to rob from us, God always purposes to prosper us. The enemy comes to *steal*; Jesus came that we may *have*. The enemy tries to *kill* us, but God's Word promises us that Jesus came to give us *life*. The devil seeks to *destroy*, but Jesus brings us *abundance*. So, we understand that while the enemy attempts daily to *steal*, *kill*, and *destroy* us, Jesus' death, burial, and resurrection assure that we have life abundantly.

God has promised us that he will keep in perfect peace whoever keeps her mind fixed on Him. (See Isaiah 26:3.) Instead of focusing on the problem, put your trust in God. Learn to trust Him by not exalting the problem and allowing it to govern your thoughts. Seek out Scriptures that relate to your situation and choose to meditate on them and memorize them. Someone once told me, "What you think about, you talk about, and what you talk about, you bring about." By intentionally changing your thought process, you can change your mind. You do this by changing your words—and the result will be a changed life.

No Place for Fear

Did you know that God is not moved by fear? Fear does not invoke God's presence. You will never find Him dwelling where fear is induced. God's place of habitation is in our praise. (See Psalm 22:3 KJV.) If you ever want God to show up on your behalf, just start praising Him. Because we often try to understand God exclusively with our intellects, we miss many opportunities to have Him in our midst.

Praise may seem too easy or an ineffective recourse if you don't have a relationship with God. If you've never taken the liberty of singing the praises of God instead of giving audience to the pressures of your thought life, then you won't understand the power of praise. *Praise is what you do both when you don't know what to do and when you do know what to do.* No matter your circumstances or emotional state, the praise of God should be continually in your mouth. Hebrews 13:15 says, *"Let us continually offer the sacrifice of praise to God, that is, the fruit of our lips, giving thanks to His name."*

You cannot praise and complain at the same time. Praise is an instrument and weapon of our warfare against the devil that is mighty through God to destroy every negative thought and the ungodly spirit that introduced the thought. (See 2 Corinthians 10:4.) God never turns a deaf ear when His children cry out for help, especially when His praise is on their lips because of their confidence that He will come through for them. (See Psalm 3:4.)

> *You cannot praise and complain at the same time.*

For this reason, praise is really the litmus test of your faith. According to *Merriam-Webster's 11th Collegiate Dictionary*, a litmus test is "a test in which a single factor (as an attitude, event, or fact) is decisive." Litmus tests can be conducted to test scientific data, political leanings, social trends, and so forth.

As a pastor, I was intrigued by a particular litmus test that was recently brought to my attention. Concerned by the number of declining and dissolving marriages in his assembly, a local pastor conducted a survey to identify the couples who were experiencing difficulties in their marriages. His purpose was to reach these troubled unions in order to help them before either spouse bailed out. This pastor concluded that couples with inconsistent church attendance must be having troubles in their marriages. His hypothesis was that a decline in consistent church attendance indicated a problematic marriage—and his theory proved largely true in his church.

Praise is the litmus test of your decision to believe in God and His promises. By praising Him, we prove our faith and hope and put them in balance. Quite simply, our praise is an expression of faith and hope in God.

Again, the psalmist expressed that God lives in the praises of His people. It is my understanding that if He lives in our praises, then that's where we should seek to find Him. There is no point in living with crippling fear, entertaining doubt, or walking in unbelief. If praising God will cause Him to come to where you are and be your *"very present help in trouble,"* as He promises to be in Psalm 46:1, then dedicate yourself to praise. Praise instills greater trust in God in your mind, putting you at peace.

Songs of Praise

[Speak] *to one another in psalms and hymns and spiritual songs, singing and making melody in your heart to the Lord.*

(Ephesians 5:19)

One way to praise God is through songs and hymns, such as the one we're about to discuss. This hymn expresses trust in God's presence despite personal tragedy.

More than a hundred years ago, Horatio Gates Spafford wrote the words to a hymn put to music by Philip Bliss that has ministered to countless individuals ever since. "It Is Well with My Soul" expresses what we should be able to say in times of comfort and calamity alike.

When peace, like a river, attendeth my way,
When sorrows like sea billows roll;
Whatever my lot, Thou hast taught me to say,
It is well, it is well, with my soul.
(Refrain)
It is well, with my soul,
It is well, with my soul,
It is well, it is well, with my soul.
(Last Verse)
And Lord, haste my day when my faith shall be sight,
The clouds be rolled back as a scroll;
The trump shall resound, and the Lord shall descend,
Even so, it is well with my soul.

This hymn was written in response to a great tragedy that befell Horatio Gates Spafford. In 1873, his wife and four daughters had been traveling by boat to England when their ship collided with another and sank. His wife survived, but his daughters did not. The words evoke the response of the

Shunammite woman to the unexpected death of her only child in 2 Kings 4:26.[1]

Spafford's lyrics express the truth that no matter what comes your way, if you are in Christ, your soul can be at peace even in the midst of adversity. You don't have to be moved by calamity. Be constant in your faith, and let nothing move you. *"Therefore, my beloved brethren, be steadfast, immovable, always abounding in the work of the Lord, knowing that your labor is not in vain in the Lord"* (1 Corinthians 15:58).

> *No matter what comes your way, if you are in Christ, your soul can be at peace even in the midst of adversity.*

---

[1] "A Hymn and Its History," www.biblestudycharts.com (accessed 7 April 2009).

12

HERE I GROW AGAIN

S ouls are a lot like trees. Just as trees require pruning, so do our souls. Some of the things we have processed in our "minds' eyes"—our souls—are tainting our perceptions in life. So, we need to allow the steady hand of the Master Arborist to cut back and trim the areas of our minds that have produced fruitless experiences and hindered healthy growth and development.

As a specialist in the cultivation and care of trees, an arborist protects each tree, preventing it from developing diseases or becoming infested by pests. The arborist is not unaccustomed to performing diagnosis, treatment, or even tree surgery. He will sever the part of any tree that is not producing or that may be decaying or withering. If he must sever something, he studies the limb or trunk, every ring of which tells a story about the history of the tree.

Like the trunk of a tree, your heart houses the history of your life, and your soul records every last detail. Thus, you reveal the stories of your life with every expression you portray. In the recesses of your mind is recorded every good thing—along with every hurt, disappointment, insult, and conflict you've ever experienced; if you live untreated from these "pests," then, like a tree infested with disease, you'll begin to decay.

In contrast, if you've been redeemed from the imperfections of your past, then your life will bloom with the fruits of victory. Like a tree that begins to flower and flourish at the hand of an arborist, so will the soul prosper when God has redeemed it from the disease of the pains of the past.

You must give attention to your soul every day and allow it to be transformed by the renewal of your mind. (See Romans 12:2.) As we meditate on the words of our heavenly Arborist and yield our wills completely to His, we allow Him to transform our minds. But if we don't submit to the Holy Spirit's leading, we run the risk of losing our souls eternally.

There are six characteristics that an arborist looks for in a healthy tree. He identifies these by asking the following questions:

1. Is the tree losing leaves?
2. Are there insects on the leaves?
3. Are the leaves turning brown?
4. Do the leaves have holes in them?
5. Are there fewer buds this year than there were last year?
6. Are the flowers blooming or not?

In the garden of your life, the Master Arborist want to make sure your soul is healthy, and His desire is for you to concentrate on developing these six attributes:

1. Keep your mind alert by feeding it information and knowledge that will develop it.
2. Make sure you are not dwelling on negative or petty thoughts.
3. Don't listen to gossip or any speech that does not promote healthy thoughts.
4. Spend less time living in the past, particularly if you tend to revisit old hurts.
5. Yield to the Holy Spirit in order to bear good fruit.
6. Trust the Master Arborist to know what is best for your growth and development. Allow Him to eradicate fear from your faith.

Fear Weakens Faith

Job said, "For the thing I greatly feared has come upon me, and what I dreaded has happened to me" (Job 3:25). Job was concerned about two things: what would come upon him and what would happen to him. A careful study of this particular book will reveal that it was fear that opened the door to both. Fear is among the most debilitating spirits that we can encounter, and it keeps us from moving forward by paralyzing us with thoughts of what could happen.

After feeding the five thousand with two fish and five barley loaves (see Matthew 14:15–21), Jesus commanded His disciples to get into a boat and cross over to the other side of the sea while He sent the multitudes of people on their ways. As the disciples traveled in the boat, a contrary wind came against

> *Fear is among the most debilitating spirits that we can encounter.*

them, tossing their boat on the water; about that time, Jesus came walking toward them on the surface of the water. Seeing Jesus but not recognizing Him, the disciples were troubled even more than they were by the waves, and they cried out in fear, *"It is a ghost!"* (See verses 22–26.)

Sometimes, when we face trouble, we can be so consumed by it that when Jesus brings us the answer (by speaking to our spirits through His Holy Spirit, for example), fear distorts our perception. Instead of believing what the Holy Spirit has spoken to us, we allow life's storms and waves to override the voices of our minds, and we become overtaken by panic.

When Jesus was approaching His disciples on the water, He said to them, *"Be of good cheer! It is I; do not be afraid"* (Matthew 14:27). Peter answered Him, saying, *"Lord, if it is You, command me to come to You on the water,"* and Jesus replied, *"Come"* (verses 28–29). Peter did as He said—he got out of the ship and walked toward Jesus. However, once he noticed the tumultuous winds, he became frightened and started to sink, crying out, *"Lord, save me!"* (verse 30).

Peter spoke with faith, but he quickly lost it to the boisterous winds. When he asked Jesus if he could come to Him, Jesus invited and enabled him to do so. But as fear overwhelmed Peter, he began to sink. Jesus answered his cries for help; He stretched forth His hand and caught Peter. (See verse 31.) Jesus was apparently concerned by Peter's low level of belief, because He said to him, *"O you of little faith, why did you doubt?"* (verse 31).

Peter doubted not only when he was walking on water, but also earlier, when Jesus was approaching the boat. At Jesus' assurance, *"Be of good cheer!*

It is I," Peter responded, *"If it is You, command me to come to You"* (Matthew 14:27–28, emphasis added). So, even though Peter seemed inclined to respond in faith, he was doubtful to walk in it. Is that really faith at all?

I am reminded of the Scripture in which Jesus lamented, *"These people draw near to Me with their mouth, and honor Me with their lips, but their heart is far from Me"* (Matthew 15:8). Responding to God with our words and not believing what we say is formalism—verbally going through the motions. *Merriam-Webster's* defines *formalism* as "the practice or the doctrine of strict adherence to prescribed or external forms." Here is what the Word of God has to say about people who practice this: they are *"having a form of godliness but denying its power"* (2 Timothy 3:5). When we allow formalism in our lives, we deny God's power.

On several occasions, Jesus reprimanded the disciples for their disbelief and formalism because it hindered God's ability to move for them. God moved repeatedly for Jesus because He trusted God's Word without question, and the result was God's power in manifestation every time He needed it. But it was not always that way with the disciples because they often failed to believe.

In another account, found in Mark 4:36–41, Jesus and His disciples were on a ship when the sea began to rage out of control, and the disciples became afraid because they did not trust God to protect them. Jesus, on the other hand, was sound asleep in the stern of the boat; which indicated His trust in God. In their distress, the disciples awakened Him, and He spoke to the storm, commanding it, *"Peace, be still!"* (verse 39). Immediately, the winds and the waves obeyed Him and became calm. God moved at the words of Jesus, but Jesus sternly rebuked the disciples, asking, *"Why are you so fearful? How is it that you have no faith?"* (verse 40).

Jesus was the Prince of Peace, but when He was asleep on the boat, He was just as much a human as were the disciples. The difference was His absolute faith and unwavering trust in God's power and ability to take care of Him.

God desires for us to have peace of mind, even in the midst of life's storms. When the waters rise and the winds grow violent—and we know that they sometimes will—remember that God has given you His peace as protection from whatever comes your way.

13

RENEWING YOUR MIND

And do not be conformed to this world, but be transformed by the renewing of your mind, that you may prove what is that good and acceptable and perfect will of God.
—Romans 12:2

Τhe apostle Paul understood the importance of transforming one's mind, a process that he knew didn't come from any goodness of his own. He attributed his steadfast faith to Jesus Christ, declaring boldly, *"I have been crucified with Christ; it is no longer I who live, but Christ lives in me; and the life which I now live in the flesh I live by faith in the Son of God, who loved me and gave Himself for me"* (Galatians 2:20). What a wonderful concept. Oh, that we would trust Christ to live through us!

God wants you—body, soul, and spirit—to take the same creative ability and ingenuity He placed within you when you were formed in your mother's womb and use it in His kingdom to minister to the needs of others. Your beauty, wit, intellect, artistry, persuasion, compassion, strength, and other qualities are all things He desires to use. And these are not just for you; rather, they are to empower others and change the world.

In all that you do, purpose to uphold Paul's exhortation from Philippians 2:3–8:

Do nothing out of selfish ambition or vain conceit, but in humility consider others better than yourselves. Each of you should look not only to your own interests, but also to the interests of others. Your attitude should be the same as that of Christ Jesus: who, being in very nature

God, did not consider equality with God something to be grasped, but made himself nothing, taking the very nature of a servant, being made in human likeness. And being found in appearance as a man, he humbled himself and became obedient to death—even death on a cross!

(NIV)

> *A renewed mind should be a welcomed change, for it means that your efforts have been transformed from filthy rags into a pure, radiant robe in Christ.*

So, am I suggesting that you die? Yes—but not literally. Die to your old nature—the sinful part of you that formerly defied God's Word. In so doing, you will renew your mind.

A renewed mind should be a welcomed change, for it means that your efforts have been transformed from filthy rags into a pure, radiant robe in Christ. And this transformation comes only by the grace of God. The prophet Isaiah said, "*We need to be saved. But we are all like an unclean thing, and all our righteousnesses arelike filthy rags*" (Isaiah 64:5–6). By "righteousnesses," he meant the good things we try to do in order to merit God's grace or to earn our own salvation. But those were like *"filthy rags."*

When we accept Christ as our Lord and Savior, our filthy rags become a radiant robe. Paul illustrated this process in the book of Colossians, saying,

> *You're done with that old life. It's like a filthy set of ill-fitting clothes you've stripped off and put in the fire. Now you're dressed in a new wardrobe. Every item of your new way of life is custom-made by the Creator, with his label on it.* (Colossians 3:9–10 MSG)

This means that apart from Christ, the fabric of who we are has little worth. Without His saving grace, our fabric is fraying fast; it won't endure. So, let's allow the Word of God and the salvation He offers to cleanse the stains of our fabric so that we can put on robes of His righteousness. Then, we will be parts of a beautiful patchwork tapestry: the church, or the bride of Christ. We will be pure and lovely because of His cleansing.

As we read in Ephesians 5:25–27,

Christ…loved the church and gave Himself for her, that He might sanctify and cleanse her with the washing of water by the word, that He might present her to Himself a glorious church, not having spot or wrinkle or any such thing, but that she should be holy and without blemish.

Fulfilling our unique roles as patches in the quilt of His people brings glory to God. And again, we are to be without blemish, for Christ died so that His bride could be spotless. "How do I accomplish that?" you might ask. By recognizing who God says in His Word that you are and consistently thinking and meditating on those things.

Finally, brethren, whatever things are true, whatever things are noble, whatever things are just, whatever things are pure, whatever things are lovely, whatever things are of good report, if there is any virtue and if there is anything praiseworthy; meditate on these things. The things which you learned and received and heard and saw in me, these do, and the God of peace will be with you. (Philippians 4:8–9)

A Nickel for Your Thoughts

The following is a list of popular expressions involving the mind. Among them may be an expression you have grown accustomed to saying or hearing. Let's use a little humor to process these phrases in a positive way.

- **"Change your mind."** Don't continue to think irrationally. Meditating on God's Word and His promises to His children will cause you to think differently.

- **"I'll give him a piece of my mind."** Stop using this expression. It seems we've given away too many pieces of our minds already. It's time to renew your mind instead.

- **"That blows my mind."** A mind is a terrible thing to waste. Don't blow your mind or waste your time.

* **"I'm losing my mind."** I believe that making this confession has caused many people to do just that. Take this expression out of your vocabulary.

* **"I need to remind myself…."** Do this daily. Remind yourself of who you are in Christ. Remind yourself that you can do all things through Him who gives you strength. (See Philippians 4:13.)

* **"I'm out of my mind."** Cast "out of your mind" every thought that negates God's Word.

* **"I've made up my mind."** Practice this principle by choosing to stay focused on God's Word as it relates to you. Don't look to the left or to the right. Stay focused with a made-up mind to do the will of God.

* **"You have a weak mind."** Remember, you are strong in the Lord and in the power of His might. You have the power of a sound mind. *"Let the weak say, 'I am strong'"* (Joel 3:10).

* **"I should have gone with my first mind."** Generally, it's a good practice to go with your first mind when making a decision. But that is good only if you practice God's Word and you don't have a second mind.

14

CONTROLLING YOUR EMOTIONS

What are emotions? *Merriam-Webster's* defines *emotion* as "the affective aspect of consciousness...; a state of feeling; a conscious mental reaction (as anger or fear) subjectively experienced as strong feeling usually directed toward a specific object and typically accompanied by physiological and behavioral changes in the body." If you are like I am, you experience the entire spectrum of feelings, often within the span of thirty days. Women are highly emotional beings, and we have our hormones to thank, in particular.

Early in my marriage, I experienced complex emotions during my menstrual cycles. My husband, Darrell, would tease me and say that I never allowed him to recover from one thirty-day period to the next. He became well-acquainted with my schedule and was able to mark on the calendar the date on which he'd have to "brace himself," as he put it. Darrell would ready himself two weeks in advance during the precycle, which would be followed by five days of my being "untouchable." So, he technically had only seven days of grace.

One night, my husband and my oldest son, DJ, were watching TV in the living room while I lay sleeping on the couch. I was trying to escape, at least for a moment, the spectrum of uncomfortable menstrual symptoms that were plaguing me—tenderness, bloating, and irritability. I was suddenly awakened by the sound of the television; I assumed, however, that the noise had been DJ talking. Impulsively, I slapped him on the side of the head and screamed, "Boy, shut up!" My husband understood my anguish, but he also recognized its desire to govern my life. Kindly but firmly, he said to me, "Don't you ever speak to our son like that again."

Sobered by my husband's words and by feelings of regret for my actions, I determined to take authority over that emotion of anger, once and for all. My disposition during my menstrual cycle was always a total departure from my true temperament, and this time, it had gone too far. Thank God for Romans 8:26, which declares, *"Likewise the Spirit also **helpeth** our infirmities"* (KJV). That night, the Holy Spirit had a little help from my husband, who had chosen to help my infirmity, too. I resolved never again to allow the dictates of my flesh to force an emotional response from me.

Since that day, I have never experienced the emotional swings and physical discomfort that are usually associated with menstruation. Darrell, DJ, and I now laugh about that night, but at the time, it was no laughing matter. Taking authority over the emotions that were triggered by my hormones liberated me from their control.

I've come to understand that a woman's period is a time of purification and cleansing. Just as the body is naturally purged and purified through menstruation, the mind needs to be cleansed of negative thinking and sour attitudes. Take note of your thoughts, attitudes, and anxieties during your cycles. I believe that doing so will make a difference in how you experience this period—and how your family members and friends experience it, as well.

Releasing Anger

Even though you won't find the word *emotion* in the Bible (unless, of course, you consult a contemporary version, such as *The Message*), you will find a host of characteristics, personalities, and expressions that define emotion. In the *New King James Version*, the emotion of *grief* is mentioned twenty-eight times, *frightened* is mentioned six times, and *sorrow* is mentioned seventy times. It is difficult to believe that *joy* is mentioned only 158 times. Exceeding this word by seventy-five, the word *anger* is an emotion that probably receives more attention than most in the Bible, occurring 233 times in the *New King James Version*.

Anger has cost people their families, their jobs, and their lives. Amazingly, anger is not necessarily a sin. Righteous anger against sin is perfectly acceptable—in fact, it's expected of us. Ephesians 4:26 commands us, *"Be angry, and do not sin,"* so we know that anger and sin are not necessarily synonymous; we can be angry and still not sin. The problem is that anger often leads to sinful behavior, such as retaliation and bitterness. God knows that we will encounter situations that will provoke our anger, but He has provided His peace and longsuffering to counter this emotion. His desire is that His children will embrace the fruit of the Spirit (see Galatians 5:22–23) and practice gentleness and patience rather than be ruled by their emotions, especially ones of rage.

> *Anger and sin are not necessarily synonymous; we can be angry and still not sin.*

"Be angry, and do not sin" means that you can be angry and leave the house. Be angry and take a drive. Be angry and call your mom, best friend, or pastor. But please, don't allow the emotion of anger to cause you to sin. Release that anger to God. Cry, if you must, but don't hang on to anger. Let it go.

I haven't listed all 233 references to anger in the *New King James Version*, but I have provided enough examples below to jumpstart your meditation on these Scriptures. By learning about godly anger and learning to practice patience and mercy, you will be equipped, when provoked, to avoid giving in to such works of the flesh as hatred and strife.

- *"Cease from anger, and forsake wrath; do not fret; it only causes harm"* (Psalm 37:8).

- *"A fool shows his annoyance at once, but a prudent man overlooks an insult"* (Proverbs 12:16 NIV).

- *"He who is slow to wrath has great understanding, but he who is impulsive exalts folly"* (Proverbs 14:29).

- *"A gentle answer turns away wrath, but a harsh word stirs up anger"* (Proverbs 15:1 NIV).

- *"A hot-tempered man stirs up dissension, but a patient man calms a quarrel"* (Proverbs 15:18 NIV).

- *"He who is slow to anger is better than the mighty, and he who rules his spirit than he who takes a city"* (Proverbs 16:32).

+ *"It is to a man's honor to avoid strife, but every fool is quick to quarrel"* (Proverbs 20:3 NIV).

+ *"Do not say, 'I'll pay you back for this wrong!' Wait for the LORD, and he will deliver you"* (Proverbs 20:22 NIV).

+ *"Mockers stir up a city, but wise men turn away anger"* (Proverbs 29:8 NIV).

+ *"A fool gives full vent to his anger, but a wise man keeps himself under control"* (Proverbs 29:11 NIV).

+ *"An angry man stirs up dissension, and a hot-tempered one commits many sins"* (Proverbs 29:22 NIV).

When you invest in your mind by instilling within it the Word of God, you prepare your heart to respond in a godly way when your anger is provoked. Controlling your emotions rather than being ruled by them is vital, as Leah learned in the account we're about to discuss.

Misplaced Motivation in Emotions

Jacob also went in to Rachel, and he also loved Rachel more than Leah. And he served with Laban still another seven years. When the LORD saw that Leah was unloved, He opened her womb; but Rachel was barren. So Leah conceived and bore a son, and she called his name Reuben; for she said, "The LORD has surely looked on my affliction. Now therefore, my husband will love me." Then she conceived again and bore a son, and said, "Because the LORD has heard that I am unloved, He has therefore given me this son also." And she called his name Simeon. She conceived again and bore a son, and said, "Now this time my husband will become attached to me, because I have borne him three sons." Therefore his name was called Levi. And she conceived again and bore a son, and said, "Now I will praise the LORD." Therefore she called his name Judah. Then she stopped bearing. (Genesis 29:30–35)

In the biblical account of Jacob and his wives Leah and Rachel, the physical attributes of Laban's daughters receive attention. Leah, the older daughter, is described as having delicate eyes, while Rachel was *"beautiful of form and appearance"* (Genesis 29:17). Jacob loved Rachel; it was her hand that he had requested in marriage. It seems safe to say that Leah never had a chance, which is why her father disguised her to trick Jacob into marrying her.

Moved with compassion when He saw that Leah was rejected, God opened her womb and enabled her to conceive. It has been said that when the Lord *opens the womb* and brings life to the broken areas of one's existence, human nature makes one nonetheless inclined to seek healing in the source of pain itself. For example, when a woman suffers physical or emotional abuse, it is not uncommon for her to cling to the source of her anguish. For some complex reason, she seeks validation from her abuser.

Leah named her first son Reuben, which means "see, a son." She believed that because God, in His grace, had given her a son, it would draw Jacob to her in love. God looked on her weakness, affliction, and insecurities, and He blessed her. Leah tried to use the birth of her sons to vie for her husband's affections—naming the next two Simeon ("to be heard") and Levi ("joined")—but to no avail.

She conceived in the wrong spirit. Even though she bore children and gave them honorable names, those names voiced her feelings concerning her marriage. Reuben, Simeon, and Levi's names amounted to pleas made to Jacob—"look at me," "hear me," and "join with me." But these pleas fell on deaf ears.

The components of human consciousness that involve feeling and sensibility, the emotions, are engaged in almost constant war against the intellect. Such was the experience of Leah. She was overwhelmed by feelings of rejection by her husband, but she eventually had the sense to realize that no number of sons could force her husband to look at her, hear her, or join himself with her. It was going to take more than a son to win her husband's affections.

By the time she bore her final son, she had learned to rejoice in the Lord's affections. She named this son Judah, which means "praise." Finally! Leah stopped

> *The components of human consciousness that involve feeling and sensibility, the emotions, are engaged in almost constant war against the intellect.*

dwelling on her emotions, which had been her motivations in having children, and rendered her affections to God, who never disappoints or neglects us. Leah learned to set her affections on things above. She renewed her mind when she cultivated her relationship with God through praise, despite her disappointment with her circumstances.

Emotions—External Actions, Internal Factors

> Stress is not a characteristic of the Holy Spirit; therefore, it is not something we are intended to manage.

Stress is related to both external and internal factors. Stress is not a characteristic of the Holy Spirit; therefore, it is not something we are intended to manage. To even suppose that you should manage stress is proof that it is actually governing you. External factors that may influence your emotions include your environment, your job, your relationships, and the expectations demanded of you on a daily basis. Internal factors that may influence your ability to handle stress include your nutrition and overall health, emotional stability, and fitness level. We need to be emotionally whole. God promises to give you His rest and peace as long as you are walking upright. You do this by meditating on His Word.

Philippians 4:6 urges us, *"Be anxious for nothing, but in everything by prayer and supplication, with thanksgiving, let your requests be made known to God."* Speak your requests, not your distress! Your confession should not be based on what you're feeling (through your senses) or how you're feeling (your emotional state), because emotional and physiological feelings can cause you to act irrationally.

Our emotions can open a doorway for Satan to gain advantage over us. You must be careful not to be consumed by your emotions. Strife is as much an emotion as it is an action. What you think is intertwined with what you do. How many times have you heard or said, "I didn't think to do that," or "I was thinking about doing..."? We can't separate ourselves from our emotions, for God created us to be emotional beings. We can, however, guard our emotions from being developed into persistent thoughts. *"Keep* your heart with all diligence, for out of it spring the issues of life" (Proverbs 4:23). We *can* cultivate positive, healthy emotions by dwelling on the Word of God and its promises to us.

Healthy Emotions

The entrance of Your words gives light; it gives understanding to the simple. (Psalm 119:130)

Positive emotions, like joy, excitement, and contentment, are befitting for the body and soul. They have healing qualities that are almost medicinal, and they provide a sense of release and relief when expressed. Happiness is a wonderful emotion.

> *Meditate on God's Word, allowing it to comfort you so that you can experience unspeakable joy full of glory.*

Make a list of all the things that bring elation to your life and try to incorporate at least one of them in your life every day. Pursue joy, for *"the joy of the* Lord *is your strength"* (Nehemiah 8:10). Meditate on God's Word, allowing it to comfort you so that you can experience unspeakable joy full of glory.

The law of the Lord *is perfect, converting the soul; the testimony of the* Lord *is sure, making wise the simple; the statutes of the* Lord *are right, rejoicing the heart; the commandment of the* Lord *is pure, enlightening the eyes; the fear of the* Lord *is clean, enduring forever; the judgments of the* Lord *are true and righteous altogether. More to be desired are they than gold, yea, than much fine gold; sweeter also than honey and the honeycomb. Moreover by them Your servant is warned, and in keeping them there is great reward. Who can understand his errors? Cleanse me from secret faults. Keep back Your servant also from presumptuous sins; let them not have dominion over me. Then I shall be blameless, and I shall be innocent of great transgression. Let the words of my mouth and the meditation of my heart be acceptable in Your sight, O* Lord, *my strength and my Redeemer.*

(Psalm 19:7–14)

15

SISTERHOOD

Chaka Khan's hit "I'm Every Woman" sounds like it would be the perfect theme song to celebrate the unity of womanhood, even though that isn't the intent of the song. It's actually a woman proclaiming her ability to be "every woman" and do anything in order to please the man in her life.

What I want to convey in this chapter, though, is what the song seems to be about—our similarities and differences, the things that we share and the things that set us apart. The sense that I'm "every woman" is evident in the compassion I feel every time I hear of a woman being hurt, mistreated, or rejected. I also rejoice with other women in their times of joy, even if I don't really know them. I have borne in prayer the burdens of every woman I've ever ministered to or befriended. In so doing, I have been fulfilling the law of Christ; as it says in Galatians 6:2, *"Bear one another's burdens, and so fulfill the law of Christ."* I feel concern and compassion for all women, regardless of age, race, class, and marital status, because I know that they all need to be made whole, regardless of their circumstances.

The fibers of our makeups are a commonality we possess. God modeled each and every one of us after the same template—His image. What distinguishes us, though, are the unique ways in which our fabrics stain

> *If we mend the tears in the fabric of our beings, individually and collectively, then we can help bring change to one another.*

and unravel. The frays of life often divide us. But if we mend the tears in the fabric of our beings, individually and collectively, then we can help bring change to one another. If, however, we continue to tear one another down rather than build one another up, we're only ripping apart the fabric of our lives as women and hindering our own purpose to cultivate and have dominion over the earth.

I have two sisters and several sisters-in-law, all whom I love very much. Each of them brings a different element to my life and adds to my creativity and purpose. They are all individual threads in the fabric of my life. If something becomes loosened in the life of any of them, it affects my fabric, and I must help to mend the area where her thread has become unraveled. If my sisters experience times of lack, troubled marriages, physical illnesses, or any other challenge, it touches my life because they are all parts of my fabric. So, I must pray for them, minister healing to them, and sow love and nurturing into them so that our fabric, as a whole, is intact.

Jesus is coming to claim a fabric—the wedding dress of His bride, the church—that is blemish-free. He's not just coming for one of us; He's coming for all of us, and He wants His whole body to be complete and flawless.

Helping Our Sisters Be Blemish-Free

Over the years, I have developed relationships with many different women, each of them as unique as the fingerprint that identifies her. Though I have had many friendships and relationships, I have only one best friend. She is so dear to me. Both of us were born in the same year, in the same city, and at the same hospital. However, we met in a completely different state far from our hometown when we were in our twenties! I'd like to think we're twins who were born on different days. What I value most about my best friend is her trustworthiness; she has never let me down. I have never met anyone else like her; she epitomizes the friend Solomon spoke about when he said that *"a friend loves at all times"* (Proverbs 17:17).

I trust her to encourage me and to correct me, because I know that she does so in love. She brings more attention to my success than I do, and she helps me to balance my life. She has always exhibited wisdom beyond her years, and I thank God for her. As my mother made her transition out of my life and into life eternal, my best friend made a transition in. Her strength, character, and wisdom remind me so much of my mom. Like my mother, she is beautiful, both without and within. She even resembles my mom, to an extent. When it comes to getting things done, she is the woman to make it happen.

I can't recall us ever disagreeing on anything, except for a satin suit of mine. I thought it was cute; she thought it was ugly. She said, "Don't even give that to anyone; throw that 'thang' away!" And I did just that.

In most relationships, conflicts are bound to arise. But it is the relationships that overcome conflicts that have the most value. So, we must cultivate our relationships. Learn to understand the purpose for which each woman in your life was put there. For example, if you have a conflict with your boss, realize that perhaps your boss is there to sharpen you and to draw greatness from you. (See Proverbs 27:17.)

> *In most relationships, conflicts are bound to arise. But it is the relationships that overcome conflicts that have the most value.*

Out of Sight, Out of Mind

You've probably heard the phrase, "Out of sight, out of mind," but have you ever really thought about it? *Out of sight, out of mind* means that something is easily forgotten or dismissed as unimportant if it isn't visible. *You've* never seen yourself. We've never seen ourselves face-to-face; every image of ourselves has been a reflection or a photograph.

My husband often says to me, "You are so beautiful." Even though I may not feel like I'm looking my best at that moment, I'll go to the mirror to see what he's complimenting because I can't see myself.

We often neglect to invest in what we don't see on a regular basis— ourselves! This is true spiritually, mentally, and bodily. Without consulting a reflective surface, such as a mirror or window, we can't know if we need to powder our noses, floss food from our teeth, or smooth the foundation on our faces. We have to trust those people near and dear to us, including our sisters in Christ, to let us know if our slips are showing, a hair is out of place, or the outfits we're wearing are too tight. In addition, we count on those same individuals to be our emotional mirrors. We need them to reflect to us our wounded spirits, sad countenances, and angry dispositions, and then to help us heal and deal.

Read this Scripture closely, for it's extremely important.

> *For if anyone is a hearer of the word and not a doer, he is like a man observing his natural face in a mirror; for he observes himself, goes away, and immediately forgets what kind of man he was. But he who looks into the perfect law of liberty and continues in it, and is not a forgetful hearer but a doer of the work, this one will be blessed in what he does.*
>
> (James 1:23–25)

If the first part of this Scripture describes you, then, in essence, you *behold, walk away,* and then *forget*. What we should be doing is looking into the mirror (the law of liberty), remembering what it says, and continuing to do what it declares. And we should also be helping others to do the same thing. The woman who embraces this principle will not forget what she has seen but will purpose to do it and, in so doing, will be blessed in everything she does.

Humility versus Judging

> *Do not judge, or you too will be judged. For in the same way you judge others, you will be judged, and with the measure you use, it will be measured to you. Why do you look at the speck of sawdust in your brother's eye and pay no attention to the plank in your own eye? How can you say to your brother, "Let me take the speck out of your eye," when all the time there is a plank in your own eye? You hypocrite, first take the plank out of your own eye, and then you will see clearly to remove the speck from your brother's eye.*
>
> (Matthew 7:1–5 NIV)

We have a tendency to see everybody else's defects and downfalls; we notice their faults in the blink of an eye. But, if we're honest, we'll admit that we can pick up on their abilities and talents just as quickly if we look closely enough and with the proper attitude. We need to change the way we look at others and change the way we see ourselves. In his book *Maximized Manhood*, Edwin Louis Cole remarked, "Most people judge others by their *actions*, and themselves by their *intentions*."[2] This has occurred for far too long.

> *We need to change the way we look at others and change the way we see ourselves.*

The Word of God tells us to love our neighbors as ourselves and to prefer them above ourselves. Treating others as we would like to be treated is a principle we should practice daily. (See Matthew 7:12.) That's the place where we all need to be—loving our sisters as ourselves, with God's Word as our mirror. We should seek to find reflections of ourselves in His Word, for if we do, it means that we're living in accordance with it. Loving our sisters encompasses helping them to become more and more like Christ.

Mirror, Mirror

As I previously stated, we have never really seen ourselves; our self-images depend on reflections. When you behold your reflection in the mirror of life, what do you see? Defeat? Triumph? The astounding thing is that although we were created in the image and likeness of God, our present likenesses—our thoughts, words, and actions—are frequently far from the images He had in mind when He created us. The primary difference lies in the fact that we are sinful, while God is completely sinless. Romans 5:20 says, *"But where sin abounded, grace abounded much more."* Sin certainly abounds in us, but through the grace of God and His righteousness, we can become like He is. That's precisely why we were created in His image. We are to be living, breathing portraits of God's goodness and grace.

---

[2] Edwin Louis Cole, *Maximized Manhood* (New Kensington, PA: Whitaker House, 1982, 2001), 99.

Our natures, abilities, and characters should be like His. So, we must purpose to abide in Him and allow His Word to be resident in us so that everything we say and do will reflect who He is in our lives and on the earth.

Often, we are more concerned with the images we see in the mirror than the degree to which we resemble our heavenly Father in our thoughts, words, and actions. We sometimes spend too much time examining our reflections in the mirror as opposed to allowing the mirror of the Word of God to develop the essence of who we really are. Embellishing our outer images is fine, but we can't stop there; we need to work from the inside out. And no one is more concerned about your image than God—your spiritual image, that is. Jesus assured us with these words:

> *Why do you worry about clothing? Consider the lilies of the field, how they grow: they neither toil nor spin; and yet I say to you that even Solomon in all his glory was not arrayed like one of these. Now if God so clothes the grass of the field, which today is, and tomorrow is thrown into the oven, will He not much more clothe you, O you of little faith?*
> (Matthew 6:28–30)

God wants us looking nice, smelling good, and living well. He wants us to be representative of Him. But it isn't enough to look the part; we must walk like He did and say what He said.

We Must Be Just like He Is

We were created to be the express image of God on earth so that those who don't know Him would find reflections in the image of God in us.

In 1 Peter 3:1–5, Peter instructed wives about how to win unsaved husbands to the Lord by submitting to them. This advice has a broader application, though, for it demonstrates the importance of speaking with words that honor God and adorning oneself not just with fine jewelry or fancy clothes but with *"the ornament of a meek and quiet spirit"* (verse 4 KJV).

> *Likewise, ye wives, be in subjection to your own husbands; that, if any obey not the word, they also may without the word be won by the*

conversation of the wives; while they behold your chaste conversation coupled with fear. Whose adorning let it not be that outward adorning of plaiting the hair, and of wearing of gold, or of putting on of apparel; but let it be the hidden man of the heart, in that which is not corruptible, even the ornament of a meek and quiet spirit, which is in the sight of God of great price. For after this manner in the old time the holy women also, who trusted in God, adorned themselves, being in subjection unto their own husbands. (KJV)

This Scripture is useful for instructing us how to minister to unbelievers as a whole. How can we minister effectively if not by our godly conduct? As ambassadors of Christ, we must purpose to represent Him and to share His love. It's essential that we live lives of purpose, centered around helping others to achieve their goals and pursue their God-given purposes.

> *As ambassadors of Christ, we must purpose to represent Him and to share His love.*

It's important that we look the part, but it's even more important that we emulate the image of the Godhead. Not every place where ministry finds us will dictate that we dress fashionably. Not everyone is interested in bling, but everyone needs to know that they have a living Savior who's a king—*the* King. So, allow the created image of Christ in you—His glory and grace—to shine through in your appearance, your conversation, and your character. The next time you behold your reflection in the looking glass of life, ask yourself this question: "Mirror, mirror, on the wall, is Christ reflected in me at all?"

INVESTING IN YOUR SPIRIT

INVESTING IN YOUR SPIRIT

*God is Spirit, and those who worship Him must worship
in spirit and in truth.*
—John 4:24

Your spirit man is who you truly are. Despite this fact, many people—Christians and unbelievers alike—go about their daily lives without being conscious of their spirits or investing in them. If you are not aware of your spirit or its function, here's a hint: it's the voice inside your innermost being that you refer to when you say, "Something told me…," or "I had a feeling…." We must allow the Holy Spirit to guide us through our human spirit; it is our sensitivity to the Holy Spirit that will give us everything we need. *"His divine power has given to us all things that pertain to life and godliness, through the knowledge of Him who called us by glory and virtue"* (2 Peter 1:3).

When we have God's Spirit, we have fellowship with Him. God communes with us when He speaks to us through the Person of the Holy Spirit. Our spirits are the only part of us that is directly connected to God. Being joined with Him in spirit is like being connected to a radio frequency.

For instance, when I turn my radio dial to Jammin' 98.3 on Sunday mornings in Milwaukee, I can expect to hear my husband on the air. I can't tune in to 97.3 and receive from him because he's not there. Likewise, when I unite with the Holy Spirit through meditation of the Word and worship, I am on the same frequency as He is.

Our spirits have to be in tune or on the same frequency as the Holy Spirit; frequently meditating, frequently worshipping, and frequently practicing the principles of God's Word. When our spirits are intertwined with the Holy Spirit, we are on the same channel, and there will be no disconnection of our own human spirits from the Holy Ghost. If our spirits are joined with His, there will be no separation or end of His Spirit in us, for we will be one. When others look at us, they will see Him in us.

16

THE ESSENCE OF YOU

The word *spirit* is a fundamental, emotional, and activating principle that determines one's character. It comprises the inherent attributes that determine an individual's moral and ethical actions and reactions. It is a quality of spirit that enables you to face danger or pain without showing fear, which is *the attribute of lacking courage*.

God never intended for us to live absent of Him. That's why He gave us a place to house His Spirit. Each one of us was created so the Holy Ghost could dwell in us. The Spirit of God comes to abide in our spirits when we receive Jesus as Lord of our lives. If we lack the discipline to develop our human spirits, how can we acquaint ourselves with God?

Start listening to the gentle voice of your own human spirit, for this is how God's Spirit gets in touch with you. As our physical bodies tie us to our biological fathers, our spirits connect us to God. He's our Father through spiritual adoption. (See Romans 8:15.) So, we must cultivate our spirits so that we can have fellowship with God and so that He can lead and guide us in truth and righteousness.

Prayer keeps your heart sensitive to the leading of the Holy Spirit and enhances your ability to hear His voice. Jesus said that the Holy Spirit would reveal things that are to come, according to John 16:13. If we learn to walk with Him in prayer, we will never be overtaken by any situation or enemy in life. The Holy Spirit is the One who has been called to help us. His purpose on the earth is to reveal, lead, and guide, and He fulfills those roles excellently when we allow Him to do so.

"*The spirit of man is the candle of the* LORD, *searching all the inward parts of the belly*" (Proverbs 20:27 KJV). No part of who we are is hidden from God. He knows everything, and it is our spirits that reveal it to Him. So, our spirits and His Spirit are an exchange of light.

From infancy, our minds and bodies are developed, growing simultaneously through every phase of life so that the development of our mind parallels the growth of our bodies. But what about the progression of our spirits? Most of us are not aware we have a spirit until it's crushed, broken, or wounded. But it is the human spirit that keeps us alive.

My mother-in-law had an experience that proves this point. While she lay unconscious from anesthetics in December 2008, the doctors reasoned that she was going to die. They had lost hope, and the prognosis was an operation that could last hours, the removal of six to ten inches of her large intestine, and a four- to six-week colostomy procedure. She was given a 10 percent change of recovery.

After the surgery, as Mom lay in the intensive care unit, she could hear the doctors saying that they did not expect her to live. But while they were expecting death, she was inwardly proclaiming life. She was unable to move her lips to articulate that she had no intention of dying, so it was her own spirit that declared, "*I shall not die, but live*" (Psalm 117:18).

When we are overcome by fatigue while running a race, faced with the pain of child-bearing, or scorned by public humiliation, it is the human spirit that sustains us so that we can cross the finish line, deliver the baby, or walk with our heads held high. When our bodies have endured the pressures of life and our minds are overtaken by grief, our spirits, which are joined to the Holy Spirit, will bring us comfort, restoration, and healing.

Adorning Your Spirit

> *Add value and substance to your life by investing in your spiritual being.*

The genuine essence of who you are is found primarily in your spirit. If you are going to be all that God desires you to be, it's imperative that you recognize this. Add value and substance to your life by investing in your spiritual being. As you are getting dressed for wherever life takes you today, make sure that you clothe your spirit man; his attire is composed of the whole armor of God, which Paul described in the book of Ephesians.

> *Put on the whole armor of God, that you may be able to stand against the wiles of the devil. For we do not wrestle against flesh and blood, but against principalities, against powers, against the rulers of the darkness of this age, against spiritual hosts of wickedness in the heavenly places. Therefore take up the whole armor of God, that you may be able to withstand in the evil day, and having done all, to stand. Stand therefore, having girded your waist with truth, having put on the breastplate of righteousness, and having shod your feet with the preparation of the gospel of peace; above all, taking the shield of faith with which you will be able to quench all the fiery darts of the wicked one. And take the helmet of salvation, and the sword of the Spirit, which is the word of God.* (Ephesians 6:11–17)

The armor of God is the protection of God, and it's made available to all who take up the cross and follow Jesus.

Use the following declaration to daily ready your spirit for the challenges you face day to day. As you are washing your face, applying makeup, or slipping into your clothes, make this declaration:

Father, thank You for providing to me Your whole armor as recorded in Ephesians 6:11–17. As I ready my body for _____ (you may add what you are getting dressed to do, i.e., go to work, school, a meeting, and so forth), I equip my spirit.

I put on the belt of truth by incorporating truth into my day, and I listen attentively for the voice of the Holy Spirit so He may speak truth to me throughout the day.

As I put on the breastplate of righteousness, I bear in mind that I have this privilege because You have made me Your righteousness in Christ Jesus. Give me the wisdom to walk in and speak Your righteousness concerning my life throughout the day.

Because You have provided me with shoes of peace, I am prepared and ready to minister peace wherever I go.

As I take unto myself the shield of faith, I am reminded that opposition will come, but the shield that I carry today will extinguish and defeat all the fiery weapons of the enemy that are formed against me so that they will not prosper.

The helmet of salvation is my protection against the thoughts, influences, suggestions, and dictates of the flesh. As I place it on my head, I thank You that I have the ability to cast down imaginations and every high thing that exalts itself against the knowledge of You and bring every thought captive to the obedience of Christ.

Though I may not have my Bible in hand, I thank You that I have hidden Your Word in my heart so that I will not sin against You, and that the sword of the Spirit, which is Your Word, gives me strength and guidance through the Person of the Holy Ghost because Your Word abides in my heart.

Adorning the Inner Man with a Meek and Quiet Spirit

What is a meek and quiet spirit? I think many of us get confused about what exactly that is. It is recorded as *"the hidden character of the heart, expressed in the imperishable beauty of a gentle and calm disposition, which is precious in the sight of God"* (1 Peter 3:4 NASB). Our heavenly Father places great value in His children who have meek and quiet spirits. It's much more than being silent or shy; it is being in control of your temperament, being gentle, and walking in forbearance even when you are provoked. Meekness empowers us to take authority over our anger and walk in its quiet strength.

> *Meekness empowers us to take authority over our anger and walk in its quiet strength.*

Though it is often confused with weakness, meekness is far from being weak. When you employ or "put on" the spirit of meekness, it actually allows you to exercise strength. A woman who practices meekness can walk away from provoking situations with a sense of accomplishment because meekness helps her to put on self-control and to rest assured that *God is in control.* The more you put it into practice, the easier it will become.

Meekness is an indestructible ornament—that's why we should wear it every day. When someone possesses the ornament of meekness, she is gentle and kind, and is neither argumentative nor rude.

Quietness is the evenness, the composure, the rest of the soul, which speaks both the nature and the excellency of the grace of meekness. The greatest comfort and happiness of man is sometimes set forth by quietness.

—Matthew Henry

17

INTERWOVEN WITH THE WORD

❧

But he answered and said, "It is written, 'Man shall not live by bread
alone, but by every word that proceeds from the mouth of God.'"
—Matthew 4:4

H ere, Jesus was saying that people should not live by natural
bread, or food, only, but by every word that God speaks, which
is recorded in the Bible. It is vitally important that your daily
life be sustained by feeding continually on the Word of God. Joshua 1:8
exhorts us, *"Do not let this Book of the Law depart from your mouth; meditate*
on it day and night, so that you may be careful to do everything written in it.
Then you will be prosperous and successful" (NIV).

Our spirits require daily attention. If they are deprived of this attention, the neglect will manifest itself in our outer man, often by fatigue and
stress. If I were to survey a sample of women, asking who in the group felt
tired and overwhelmed, the majority of the women would respond affirmatively. However, if I asked that same group who among them was committed to daily feeding on the Word of God, only a few would avow their com-
mitment to feeding daily on God's Word. I believe this neglect of spiritual
growth is a primary source of stress and fatigue for many women.

Sitting at the Feet of Jesus

When we set ourselves apart daily for the purpose of sitting at the
feet of Jesus, allowing His Word to nourish us as we fellowship with Him,
strength and grace are released in our spirits. By His love and mercy, God

gives us everything that we need. We need God's grace for today. Jesus set the precedent of asking His Father to give us the things that we need for today when He taught His disciples to pray, *"Give us this day our daily bread"* (Matthew 6:11).

The Word of God is vital to our spiritual and natural survival. There simply is no other means by which we can receive the overflow of God's love, grace, direction, and strength. The greatest example of this is found in the tenth chapter of Luke, when Jesus went to visit Mary and Martha.

> *Now it happened as they went that He entered a certain village; and a certain woman named Martha welcomed Him into her house. And she had a sister called Mary, who also sat at Jesus' feet and heard His word. But Martha was distracted with much serving, and she approached Him and said, "Lord, do You not care that my sister has left me to serve alone? Therefore tell her to help me." And Jesus answered and said to her, "Martha, Martha, **you are worried and troubled about many things. But one thing is needed, and Mary has chosen that good part, which will not be taken away from her."***
>
> (Luke 10:38–42, emphasis added)

Martha can be seen to represent the countless women who don't know when to lay aside their daily chores and sit at the feet of the Master.

Jesus noticed that Martha was *"careful and troubled"* by the very thing she loved doing the most. Martha and Mary were both skilled at serving, but Martha had taken her ability to serve and valued it more than her ability to receive. The word *careful* means "caring or providing for," and the word *troubled* means "troubled in the mind." Martha was concerned more with the tasks she had to accomplish. She had a good heart; she had simply positioned her priorities wrong. God must be first, and by spending time in His Word, we give Him the opportunity to speak to us and to nourish our spirits.

Mary wasn't perfect, but she understood the importance of receiving from God. *The Message* Bible says that Mary had chosen *"the main course, [which] won't be taken from her."* Martha was serving meals, but Jesus said that spending time at His feet was the main course in life.

The one thing that was needed, Mary was wise enough to choose; sitting at the feet of Jesus and listening to His words. What Mary did is what every one of us has the privilege of doing—sitting, listening, feeding. What happens when we sit at the feet of Jesus? We are blessed.

> *What happens when we sit at the feet of Jesus? We are blessed.*

We are often like Martha. We devote ourselves to accomplishing so many things, sometimes at the expense of our relationships with God. We don't have time to commune with Him or to read His Word today because we're busy worrying about the things we have to do tomorrow. So, let's not focus on tomorrow, for in reality, we'll never get there. Think about it: today is the present. When we reach tomorrow, it will be today. What does this reveal? That God wants us to focus on what He has made available to us right now.

In her poem "Footprints in Your Heart," Eleanor Roosevelt included this now-popular phrase: "Yesterday is history. Tomorrow is mystery. Today is a gift. That's why it's called the present." If you take care of today, tomorrow will care of itself. Matthew 6:34 says, *"Do not worry about tomorrow, for tomorrow will worry about its own things."*

Use what God has given you in His Word and feed on it today. After all, Psalm 118:24 states, *"This is the day which the LORD hath made; we will rejoice and be glad in it."* God wants us to rejoice and live out today. He gives us daily bread and daily mercies which are new every morning. (See Lamentations 3:23; Matthew 6:11.) So, don't waste today thinking about yesterday. Don't miss today waiting for tomorrow.

18
PRAYER LIFE

I t is difficult to talk about ways to invest in yourself without talking about prayer. Prayer is among the most valuable investments you can make in your life. In Luke 18:1, Jesus said *"that men always ought to pray and not lose heart"* (emphasis added). *The Message* Bible says, *"Jesus told them…that it was necessary for them to pray consistently and never quit."* And in 1 Thessalonians 5:17, Paul exhorted us, *"Pray without ceasing."* So, according to the Word of God, we are never to stop praying. It is important to set aside quality time to spend in conversation with our heavenly Father every day.

A key setting aside time to commune with Father is to first believe that praying is neither a chore nor a task on the unending to-do list, and that it's not complicated. Prayer is simply talking with God so everyone is able to engage in prayer. Don't be concerned with *saying the right words* or *using the proper format*. Prayer involves sharing your heart with God and releasing to Him your worries and frustrations, your joys and triumphs and allowing Him to speak to you and give you direction concerning those very things. Prayer is a privilege and there should be a longing in every woman's heart to pray. Because of Jesus Christ, prayer is something that we *get* to do.

The Simplicity of Prayer

Prayer is not complicated. Here is a simple truth I desire to share with the body of Christ: although words are powerful, our prayers don't require eloquent words in order for God to hear them. Quite simply, our prayers should have two components: faith and sincerity of heart. I've always kept my prayers simple, and God has honored that.

My husband, Darrell, used to work at General Mitchell Field, an airport in Milwaukee, Wisconsin. On July 17, 1981, while he was at work, Darrell was struck by lightning. He was pronounced dead after forty-five minutes of unsuccessful attempts to revive him. The airport announced that three people had been struck by lightning that day. When a coworker of his named Teddie learned that Darrell Hines was one of them, she purposed to get to him.

Teddie was a Baptist. She wore bright red lipstick, vibrant nail polish, and pants. (Having been raised in the strict Holiness, I believed that such a woman couldn't possibly know God, let alone be able to get a prayer through to Him.) But her tenacity to see my husband's life revived ministered volumes to me. She was a prayerful woman of great faith. She knew God, and she knew how to pray. When Darrell was pronounced dead, Teddie simply prayed, "God, I know You're not finished with him yet. Give him his life back."

When the paramedics had determined there was nothing more they could do, they put away the defibrillators and transported Darrell to the hospital. Teddie rode along in the ambulance, believing God for a miracle. She later reported that she first felt a warm, soothing heat in the ambulance, followed by a sudden, deep breath from my husband. Though he had regained consciousness, his brain had been deprived of oxygen for a significant amount of time, which led the doctors to conclude that he would spend the remainder of his days in a vegetative state. By this point, Darrell was screaming like a caged animal, and the doctors also said that if this continued for longer than three hours, he would be like that for the rest of his life.

Hours later, Darrell had stopped screaming out; he now groaned over and over again within himself, "Lord, save me," "Bless my soul," "I can't believe this happened to me," and "Momma, help me." As he repeated those phrases again and again, he fell asleep. When he awakened, he had amnesia and couldn't remember anything. The next time he fell asleep, I prayed a prayer, but it wasn't long and drawn-out. I simply said, "Lord, when he wakes up, if he doesn't know anyone else, let him know me." As soon as Darrell opened his eyes again, his words were, "Hey, honey!" My husband knew who I was. What a wonderful answer to a brief, simple prayer!

Don't Get Caught Up in Position or Posture

Effective prayer does not require getting on your knees. Your posture during prayer is not at all as important as the content and sincerity of your prayers. Going into our prayer closets is important, but if prayer is to be constant, then we have to be found praying on every occasion, no matter where we find ourselves. After all, Daniel prayed three times a day looking out of a window (see Daniel 6:10), David prayed while in bed (see Psalm 63:6), the Israelites prayed in the middle of a battle (see 2 Chronicles 13:14), and Jonah prayed in the belly of a fish (see Jonah 2:1–9).

> *Effective prayer does not require getting on your knees.*

And your prayers can be brief. You may be cooking breakfast, driving your car, grocery shopping, or entering a board meeting and simply utter, "Lord, give me wisdom," "Lord, protect my family," "Lord, heal my body," or "Lord, give me strength."

For the majority of my life, I've made a practice of praying simple prayers and watching God answer them. I encourage you not to make prayer a complicated thing. Just open your heart to God and give Him the right of entry to your life. Then, watch as He transforms you completely.

Praying the Word of God

Every woman can have a dynamic prayer life. The key is to make sure that what you pray is prayed in faith, and that your requests align with the Word of God.

If any of you lacks wisdom, let him ask of God, who gives to all liberally and without reproach, and it will be given to him. But let him ask in faith, with no doubting, for he who doubts is like a wave of the sea driven and tossed by the wind. For let not that man suppose that he will receive anything from the Lord; he is a double-minded man, unstable in all his ways. (James 1:5–8)

The Word of God is of great importance in the act of praying. It's imperative to incorporate the Word of God in your prayer life because everything

> *Eloquence isn't necessary in approaching God in prayer, but concise application of His Word is.*

that we desire from God should be based upon His Word and His promises therein. Remember, eloquence isn't necessary in approaching God in prayer, but concise application of His Word is.

In Philippians 4:19, He promised to supply all of our need, according to His riches in glory. In Proverbs 4:22, He promised that His Word would be medicine to all of our flesh. In John 10:10, He promised to give us abundant life. In Acts 16:31, He assured us of salvation for our households.

Make certain though that you continually praise and offer thanksgiving to God. "*Therefore by Him let us continually offer the sacrifice of praise to God, that is, the fruit of our lips, giving thanks to His name*" (Hebrews 13:15). All the promises in the Word of God are Yes and Amen (see 2 Corinthians 1:20), so there is nothing that we can ever desire that God has not already made provision for.

It isn't a matter of memorizing long passages of Scripture. Simply check the topical index at the back of your Bible, where you will be directed to Scriptures related to your specific need or situation. In my book *A Wife's Prayer*, every prayer I rendered therein was inspired by Scripture. One of the most effective methods of prayer is simply taking a Scripture that speaks about what's troubling you and praying to God, thanking Him for the victory you're promised by that Scripture.

For instance, if you are working on a project and you feel inadequate to get the job done, refer to Philippians 4:13, which states, "*I can do all things through Christ who strengthens me.*" Realize that when you depend on Christ, you are strengthened for the job. When you pray in accordance with the Scripture, you are praying God's Word over the matter. Pray, "Father, I thank You for enabling me to do all things through Christ who strengthens me. Thank You for strengthening me to complete this project. Thank You for giving me the wisdom to execute it before the deadline. In Jesus' name, amen."

When we take advantage of the written Word of God by bringing it into our daily prayers, it causes them to go from mundane to dynamic.

God responds to His Word, so when we pray the Word of God, we are guaranteed an answer.

James 5:16 says, *"The effective, fervent prayer of a righteous man avails much."* The *Amplified Bible* puts it this way: *"The earnest (heartfelt, continued) prayer of a righteous man makes tremendous power available [dynamic in its working]."* But what is the power that makes our prayers effective? The answer is the power of faith in the Word of God. Through the power of faith, you can move mountains. (See Matthew 17:20; 21:21.) This is why Satan wants you to think that prayer is complicated and thus give up praying. He doesn't want the power of God to be manifested in your life. So, he deceives us and lies to us, giving us the impression that prayer is hard. But this is an absolute falsehood.

> *When we use God's words instead of our own, we are able to get to the heart of a matter without drawing from a carnal perspective.*

When we use God's words instead of our own, we are able to get to the heart of a matter without drawing from a carnal perspective. God knows everything, and within the wisdom of His Word can be found the answers to all of life's challenges, questions, and queries.

Start Each Day by Seeking God

The LORD will perfect that which concerns me; Your mercy, O LORD, endures forever; do not forsake the works of Your hands.
(Psalm 138:8)

As a young woman, I learned to pray by giving God the very top of my day. I find it easier to engage in prayer when the hustle and bustle of the day has yet to begin. I believe King David felt the same way, because he addressed God by saying, *"Early will I seek You"* (Psalm 63:1). When we honor God with the first portion of our days, it gives Him an advantage in our lives that Satan doesn't have. There are so many voices that try to gain access to our thought lives on a day-to-day basis, and it's vital that we still ourselves and give first place to the voice of God. If we do this, His voice becomes the first voice of influence in our day.

Praying Continually Keeps Us Reliant on God for Everything

Prayer keeps God involved in the intricacies of your day-to-day life. It gives Him access to all that you engage in. Proverbs 3:5–6 tells us to trust and acknowledge God in all of our ways, and He will give direction to our paths. Imagine what our days would be like if we daily acknowledged God and allowed Him to give us guidance. As believing women, we must live our lives in a way that gives God complete access to all that we do and defers to His will and guidance. Without Him, we have only our own wisdom and strength to draw on, and we know from experience that those are limited.

In order to make a positive, lasting impact on our lives and others, we have to give time to the Father. All the help and support that our families require can be found in Him. God wants you to depend on Him for everything. He desires to be involved in every project, endeavor, challenge, and relationship that occupies your time, thoughts, or efforts. If it concerns you, it concerns Him. If it's important to you, it's important to Him. But you have to let Him in, and you do so through the portal of your prayer life.

> *If it concerns you, it concerns God. If it's important to you, it's important to Him.*

Sometimes, situations seem chaotic, but when you bring them before God in prayer, He makes the way clear. He removes all confusion and anxiety and gives you the greatest sense of peace so that you can make wise, sound decisions, or what I like to call "God decisions."

It's time for us to trust Him completely. When we choose to trust God, we strengthen the fabric of who we are. No matter what our circumstances may be, we can trust the Father. He loves us and is concerned about everything that touches our lives. So, when talking to Him in prayer, expect that confidence will arise in your heart, and learn to trust Him with your relationships, your career, and your finances. The Lord can be trusted to perfect, or to bring to completion, everything that we entrust to His care.

Steadfast in Prayer

To illustrate to His disciples the importance of praying without giving up, Jesus told a story that is known as the parable of the widow and the unjust judge. (See Luke 18:1–8.) A certain judge didn't know God and therefore did not fear Him. He also had little regard for other people. One day, a widowed woman came seeking justice from her adversary—and she wouldn't take no for an answer. Time and again, the judge refused to grant her request, yet she persisted in presenting her demands to the judge. Finally, the judge said to himself, *Even though I don't fear God or care about anyone, this woman keeps bothering me, so I might as well see that she gets what she deserves. I don't want her to wear me out by constantly bringing her problem to me.* Her persistence paid off, and the judge granted her request.

Jesus concluded the parable by telling His disciples, *"And shall God not avenge His own elect who cry out day and night to Him, though He bears long with them? I tell you that He will avenge them speedily"* (Luke 18:7–8). If an unjust judge gave justice to a widow, how much more will God, a righteous judge, reward us when He finds us faithful? Through prayer, we present our requests to God, and we simply wait on Him to answer.

At the very end of the parable, Jesus asked, *"Nevertheless, when the Son of Man comes, will He really find faith on the earth?"* (verse 8). Like the widow, we must present our requests continually to God, having faith that He will answer us. Philippians 4:6 exhorts us, *"Be anxious for nothing, but in everything by prayer and supplication, with thanksgiving, let your requests be known to God."*

The Exemplary Prayer Life of Jesus

When Jesus came to live on earth for thirty-three years, He took on a human form. As a Man, He had to eat, sleep, and rest. He was not operating on the earth as the second Person of the Trinity but as a Man who, after spending an important amount of time in prayer, was graced for His particular task. It is important to note that prayer preceded His every activity.

> *It is important to note that prayer preceded Jesus' every activity.*

Jesus prayed just before launching His ministry on earth. (See Mark 1:35.) He spent the entire night in prayer prior to choosing His disciples. (See Luke 6:12.) He prayed when he raised Lazarus from the dead (see John 11:41–42) and during and after the feeding of the five thousand. (See Matthew 14:13, 23.) He prayed when the crucifixion was imminent (see John 17:1–26), before His arrest in the garden of Gethsemane (see Luke 22:39–46), and then on the cross. (See Luke 23:34, 46.) Jesus was busy, but never too busy to pray.

Jesus always prayed before making a decision or dealing with people. Spending significant time with the Father was important to Him. He recognized His need for God's direction and wisdom; therefore, prayer played a major role in His life.

The Bible says that Jesus had the Spirit without measure or limit. (See John 3:34.) I believe that one key to maintaining an unlimited level of spirituality was the strength of Jesus' prayer life. He gave Himself to God in prayer, and because of His submission to God's plans and purposes, *"God anointed Jesus of Nazareth with the Holy Spirit and with power, who went about doing good and healing all who were oppressed by the devil, for God was with Him"* (Acts 10:38).

> *By walking with God through prayer, Jesus was able to receive all the grace and power necessary to bless every person who came across His path.*

Every day of His earthly life, Jesus had enough grace, power, and anointing to fulfill and accomplish whatever tasks were before Him. By walking with God through prayer, Jesus was able to receive all the grace and power necessary to bless every person who came across His path. He never had to send one person away. There was all-sufficiency in Him because he had been with God before ministering. Prayer gives you access to the same power and anointing that was available to Jesus.

God was able to anoint Jesus with everything He needed to minister to people because Jesus willingly submitted Himself to the Father in prayer, saying, in the garden of Gethsemane, *"Not My will, but Yours, be done"* (Luke 22:42). That should be our prayer also.

To minister effectively to others, we must first see the importance of communing with the Father in prayer. When you seek God in prayer, He fills your life with grace. You may not know in the natural how to fix a situation, but the Lord knows everything, and He will empower you with His wisdom so that you can respond effectively and deal rightly with everyone you interact with from day to day.

Never Too Busy to Pray

Jesus is our greatest example in life. As He invested in His prayer life, so should we. I can't imagine what my life would be like if I didn't make time to pray. Life comes at you fast, and when you walk in the office of a pastor, it comes at light speed. So, my prayer time goes beyond praying for myself, my husband, and our children. The people my husband and I pastor are also included in my prayer list.

I'm certain we all have experienced crisis situations that found us ill-prepared, times when we've received a call or were in a position to act but didn't know what to do. If we will make the time to enter into worship and go before the throne room of God and pray daily, we will be more prepared when times of crisis come. When those times appear and we're where we should be in prayer, we find comfort knowing that there is no problem too hard for God. The truth is, our prayer lives seem to increase in those times of great trouble, which draw us to the point where we hinge on every word or unction that God delivers to our spirits through His Spirit.

> *There is no problem too hard for God.*

When we cultivate our prayer lives, we don't have to wait on an answer; it is revealed by God's Spirit, and we know this because we have been in constant fellowship with Him, hallelujah! First Corinthians 2:9–10 says, *"Eye has not seen, nor ear heard, nor have entered into the heart of man the things which God has prepared for those who love Him. But God has revealed them to us through His Spirit. For the Spirit searches all things, yes, the deep things of God."*

Revelation comes when we spend time in prayer and fellowship with God. He reveals to us how to pray and provides the answers to our situations. When someone comes to me and needs healing in her body, I can say, by the authority and power of the Holy Ghost, that it's already done. Many times, while someone is yet speaking with me about a problem, God reveals to me the answer because I have entered His presence in prayer long before meeting with her. In my prayer time, I may have been praying in general, for the membership of Christian Faith Fellowship Church, for marriages, or for women; yet, in my times of prayer, I am careful to simply thank God for what He has done, what He is doing, or what is He is going to do. Time spent in His presence empowers me and builds me up spiritually so that when a problem confronts me, a resolve comes from my spirit because God has revealed it by His Spirit! Isn't that wonderful?

You may say, "I'm not a pastor and I don't have to minister to other people. Why should I spend time in prayer?" To receive direction, insight, and clarity for your own life.

A member of our church was recently laid off. She told me that on the day she was laid off, she had been talking to the Father about her job during her morning commute. She had said, "Father, if they give me two weeks' severance pay, I will be just fine." At that time, she had no idea that the company where she was employed would be laying off a group of individuals that day. At the close of the business day, various supervisors began calling their employees in to let them know that their positions were being eliminated. When this woman heard from her supervisor, she went to his office and was told, "Because you have been here less than a year, we wouldn't ordinarily offer you severance pay, but because this layoff is immediate, we wanted you to have a severance package. So, look over it and let me know if you'll accept it." The woman looked over the packet and saw that she would be given the equivalent of two weeks' pay. To that, she said, "Thank You, Father. But, You know, I should have asked for more."

Entering into prayer with God prepared this woman for a layoff even when she had no idea it was coming. Everyone else who was being released was devastated, but the peace of God rested on this woman, and that which would transpire that day came out of her spirit when she was in prayer that morning!

19

THE POWER OF POSITIVE WORDS

If you search the Bible—the New Testament, in particular—you will find that everything we receive from God, we receive by using our words. Words play a vital part in our successes in life; our words have power and magnitude. God is the One who sanctioned words to produce in the earth after they had been spoken. In the beginning, God spoke the world into being; everything was created as He proclaimed its existence. (See Genesis 1:1–30.) It was God's design to place power in our words. Since God Himself operates this way, and we are made in His image, it's one of His qualities that we emulate.

One of the most powerful investments that you can make in your own life is the investment of positive words. First and foremost, come to understand that you were created in the image and likeness of God, and everything He made was good. Allow this fact to keep you from looking in the mirror and speaking contrarily about yourself. Change your confession and speak only what the Word of God says about you. Every word you have spoken about yourself, and every word spoken by someone else about you that you have received, has created who you have become. Start today to be careful of what comes out of your mouth about yourself, and do not allow anyone to speak anything over your life that does not agree with God's Word.

Your words will either add to your life or take away from it, depending on where you release them and who you allow to speak into your life. You can actually have what you say about yourself. Any victories, accomplishments, or success I have received in life have been the results of what I have spoken. In order to create a desirable life, you will have to keep watch over your words. The fabric of your life can be damaged if you fail to choose your words wisely.

Should you reach a point of absolute frustration, speak words that will liberate you from those perplexities. You can expect to have a healthy body if you speak healing. You can experience peace in your home if you call it forth. Proverbs 18:21 says, *"Death and life are in the power of the tongue, and those who love it will eat its fruit."* This means that the words you speak (meditate on) will manifest in your life. In essence, what you say is what you get.

> When you begin to pronounce over and over again life-giving words that are scripturally based, then you will begin to walk in the fruit of your words.

The words that you speak shape your self-image, influencing how you think about yourself. Begin declaring that you have been fearfully and wonderfully made. When you begin to pronounce over and over again life-giving words that are scripturally based, then you will begin to walk in the fruit of your words—they will produce life!

If you want a strong marriage, speak it; if you want your business to excel, say it; if you desire a promotion, call it forth. Cease from speaking the problem; find out what God is saying in His Word and what He speaks to you in your time of prayer and begin to declare your victory, in Jesus' name!

As you gain confidence in speaking God's Word over your own life, begin to declare it in the lives of others. Speak to your relationships, especially those of your family members and particularly if you have children. If you are a mother, never cease to build your children's esteem by making declarations over their lives and having them commit those declarations to daily confessions in their own lives. As an unspoken principle, husbands depend on their wives to encourage them with words of comfort. Sometimes, all a husband needs is to hear his wife tell him how much she appreciates him, and how witty, intelligent, and resourceful he is. If you're a supervisor, celebrate your staff when they are doing well, and if you're an employee, express to your supervisor your appreciation for having the opportunity to work with her. We must use our words to work for us and to minister to others. In Proverbs 4:20–22, we have these words of exhortation: *"My son, give attention to my words; incline your ear to my sayings. Do not let them depart from your eyes; keep them in the midst of your heart; for they are life to those who find them, and health to all their flesh."*

The Word of God brings automatic comfort, so when we make declarations based upon God's Word, we have what we say, and nothing anyone else says can nullify our words.

> *The Word of God brings automatic comfort, so when we make declarations based upon God's Word, we have what we say, and nothing anyone else says can nullify our words.*

Your Words Affect Your Spirit

Proverbs 15:4 attests to the power of words, saying, *"A wholesome tongue is a tree of life, but perverseness in it breaks the spirit."* The Message Bible says it this way: *"Kind words heal and help; cutting words wound and maim."*

Again, your tongue has the ability to release death or life (see Proverbs 18:21)—it just depends on which of the two you give place to. The choice you make will minister to every part of you—spirit, soul, and body.

Your words can alter your destiny; they are the vehicles by which you obtain everything God has for you. Your words affect your spirit, for by them, you receive salvation and eternal life. As Paul wrote in Romans 10:10, *"It is with your heart that you believe and are justified, and it is with your mouth that you confess and are saved"* (NIV). Your words will take you from spiritual death to spiritual life.

By using your words to confess your sins to God and ask for His forgiveness, you are able to walk in and maintain your relationship with the Father. *"If we confess our sins, He is faithful and just to forgive us our sins and to cleanse us from all unrighteousness"* (1 John 1:9).

Your Words Affect Your Soul

Proverbs 18:20 says, *"Words satisfy the mind as much as fruit does the stomach; good talk is as gratifying as a good harvest"* (MSG). The words that you speak will affect the condition of your soul. They will either ensure that you have a healthy soul or reveal that your soul is weak and unhealthy.

The right words—*"good talk"*—satisfy the mind, which relates closely with the will and emotions, and all of these compose the soul. However, the converse is also true: wrong words and negative talk bring dissatisfaction to our minds, wills, and emotions. Words—whether good or bad, positive or negative—influence our ways of thinking.

> *God wants the words from His mouth to be the words that influence and shape our souls, for His words are good, pure, and right.*

God wants the words from His mouth to be the words that influence and shape our souls, for His words are good, pure, and right. Romans 12:2 instructs you to *"be transformed by the renewing of your mind"* in order to *"prove what is that good and acceptable and perfect will of God."* This transformation is important, and it takes place only when we yield our ways of thinking to God's way of thinking, which we learn through His words.

Much of our thinking is a collection of words that we hear others speak and retain in our minds. In the same way, we can create our thoughts by what we say. Speaking aloud God's promises from passages of Scripture will instill those promises in your mind, enabling you to think on them and recall them when tempted to doubt or fear. False or negative words can have the same effect; they can get lodged within our minds and become especially hard to eradicate. Never allow someone else's words to determine how you think of yourself or dictate what you're supposed to look like. Avoid assimilating the thoughts of someone else by resisting the temptation to repeat them yourself. The words of your mouth can have a significant impact on your emotions; positive words will make you rejoice, while negative words will make you dejected. *"Anxiety in the heart of man causes depression, but a **good word** makes it glad"* (Proverbs 12:25, emphasis added).

It is important for you, as a woman, to have a healthy soul, so you have to make sure you aren't speaking words that contradict the Word of God.

Your Words Affect Your Body

We all desire strong, healthy bodies, for they are temples of the Lord. (See 1 Corinthians 3:16.) God's Word will produce health and healing for the physical body. The Lord spoke through the prophet Joel, saying, *"Let the weak say, 'I am strong'"* (Joel 3:10). Why did He say that? Because He wanted to emphasize the power we possess in our own words. If you can say with your mouth, "I'm strong," this proclamation can produce strength in your physical body.

Many Scriptures speak of the power of words to heal. Proverbs 12:18 says, *"There is one who speaks like the piercings of a sword, but the tongue of the wise promotes health."* Recognizing that words will affect every part of you should help you understand how essential it is to place God's words in your heart and to speak them from your mouth. God's words are powerful, and they affect your spirit, soul, and body.

Move Forward

Each day, we must use the words of our mouths to help build our spirits, renew our minds, and strengthen our bodies. If we speak God's words over our lives, His creative power will work continually within us, restoring and renewing us. The woman with the issue of blood in the ninth chapter of Matthew touched Jesus in a way that drew creative power out of Him; the result was an instant manifestation of healing. Prior to touching Jesus, the woman had said to herself, *"If only I may touch His garment, I shall be made well"* (Matthew 9:21). It was the words from her mouth and the faith in her heart that activated the creative power of Jesus. Her touch tapped into the healing power in Jesus, and it all began with the words of her mouth.

Use your words to create a life of blessing for you, your family members, your friends, and those you influence. Don't use your words in a way that is not beneficial to the hearer. Psalm 64:8 says, *"He will make them [the wicked] stumble over their own tongue."* It is possible for your own words to turn against you and destroy you. Don't let this be your case. Use your words to create a life of abundance, peace, and joy.

> *Use your words to create a life of abundance, peace, and joy.*

Move out into the things of God by using your words to propel yourself into all that God has for you. He has a rich life planned for you, and He wants the words that you speak to produce fruit so you can impact the lives of others.

Avoid Corrupt Communication

Positive words produce positive results; negative words produce negative results. You cannot pick a good piece of fruit from a bad tree, and Jesus used this metaphor to explain a principle about our speech. He said,

> *For a good tree does not bear bad fruit, nor does a bad tree bear good fruit. For every tree is known by its own fruit. For men do not gather figs from thorns, nor do they gather grapes from a bramble bush. A good man out of the good treasure of his heart brings forth good; and an evil man out of the evil treasure of his heart brings forth evil. For out of the abundance of the heart his mouth speaks.* (Luke 6:43–45)

Bad trees produce bad fruit. Let your words be seasoned with love and grace, not death, in accordance with Paul's admonition from Colossians 4:6: *"Let your speech always be with grace, seasoned with salt, that you may know how you ought to answer each one."*

Paul wrote in Ephesians 4:29, *"Let no corrupt word ["communication"* KJV] *proceed out of your mouth, but what is good for necessary edification, that it may impart grace to the hearers."*

The word *corrupt* means "unfit for use; rotten or putrefied." Our words should be just the opposite, for corrupt communication is completely inappropriate for godly women. The image of seasoning one's speech with salt, as Paul introduced in Colossians 4:6, is an apt one. To me, meat always tastes better with a sprinkling of seasoning salt. We use salt to enhance the flavors of many meals we prepare. If a dish is bland and flavorless, it is less likely that people will eat it, let alone enjoy it. But if a dish is seasoned just right, they'll often come back asking for more.

Some women forfeit their opportunities to invest in others because their tongues are too sharp. Because they fail to season their words with *"salt"*—love, grace, compassion, and patience—their words are harsh and difficult for others to receive. When you speak to someone, he or she should never feel emotionally battered or torn to shreds. Those to whom you speak should afterward feel edified and encouraged in their spirits, not downtrodden and disheartened.

> *Some women forfeit their opportunities to invest in others because their tongues are too sharp.*

Let the words from your mouth minister grace and hope to those with whom you speak. I realize that we all experience times of frustration—and that's when we must be especially careful with our words. Don't say anything that you will later regret. The book of Proverbs contains a wealth of wisdom on this subject. In particular, we must heed the following precepts:

+ "He who is slow to wrath has great understanding, but he who is impulsive exalts folly" (Proverbs 14:29).
+ "A soft answer turns away wrath, but a harsh word stirs up anger" (Proverbs 15:1).
+ "A man's wisdom gives him patience; it is to his glory to overlook an offense" (Proverbs 19:11 NIV).

When your temper flares up, wait to say anything until you've calmed down. Never speak out of your anger or emotions. We must do as James exhorted—"be...swift to hear, slow to speak, slow to wrath" (James 1:19). Pray for help in controlling your tongue and taming your emotions, for an angry woman can inflict great damage, even on those she loves the most. Being quick to speak anger will cost you.

Use Your Tongue to Speak Life

Has it ever seemed to you that you weren't accomplishing anything? Have you ever felt like your life was going nowhere? Most of us have felt this way at one time or another. In those times, however, we must remind ourselves that our outlooks are never to be predicated on how we feel or on our current circumstances but rather on what we know to be true, based upon the Word of God.

The prophet Ezekiel found himself in the middle of a desert with nothing but dry bones around him. The desert represents a place of isolation, loneliness, and desolation. Many of us have taken "trips to the desert." We've experienced hurts, pains, tragedies, and pitfalls, only to be left with deep senses of despair.

But we have to learn, as Ezekiel did, that regardless of the circumstances in our lives, if we speak the Word of God and act in accordance with it, we will resurrect life in our places of dryness.

The hand of the LORD *came upon me and brought me out in the Spirit of the* LORD, *and set me down in the midst of the valley; and it was full of bones. Then He caused me to pass by them all around, and behold, there were very many in the open valley; and indeed they were very dry. And He said to me, "Son of man, can these bones live?" So I answered, "O Lord* GOD, *You know." Again He said to me, "Prophesy to these bones, and say to them, 'O dry bones, hear the word of the* LORD! *Thus says the Lord* GOD *to these bones: "Surely I will cause breath to enter into you, and you shall live. I will put sinews on you and bring flesh upon you, cover you with skin and put breath in you; and you shall live. Then you shall know that I am the* LORD.""' *So I prophesied as I was commanded; and as I prophesied, there was a noise, and suddenly a rattling; and the bones came together, bone to bone. Indeed, as I looked, the sinews and the flesh came upon them, and the skin covered them over; but there was no breath in them. Also He said to me, "Prophesy to the breath, prophesy, son of man, and say to the breath, 'Thus says the Lord* GOD: *"Come from the four winds, O breath, and breathe on these slain, that they may live."""' So I prophesied as He commanded me, and breath came into them, and they lived, and stood upon their feet, an exceedingly great army.*

(Ezekiel 37:1–10)

Can you speak life? Are you willing, as Ezekiel was when God instructed him, to use the words of your mouth to bring life back to a place in your experience where death has taken over? The Bible says that Ezekiel was carried by the Lord into this valley—the lowest point of a region. In a figurative sense, a valley can symbolize a place of depression or feelings of insignificance—feelings most of us have had to deal with at some point in our lives. But God carried Ezekiel to the valley—a place of depression—and used him to speak life to it.

There are times in our existence when God will cause us to revisit dead places that were once bursting with life. He doesn't want any aspect of our lives to be desolate or devoid of life. Don't ignore God when He leads you to look at yourself in order to acknowledge the areas that you have allowed to wither or die, for in these places, your dreams and visions can be resurrected with His supernatural power.

Ezekiel was in an open valley, which means it wasn't a hidden place. His presence there was no secret. God set him in the middle of the valley full of dry bones, which represents those dead things that had an abundance of life at an earlier time. Many women have "dry bones" in their lives because they have worked themselves to places of utter despair; though they once were vibrant and full of life, they now need God to breathe His life back into them. We all have at least one "valley of dry bones" in our lives, but thank God, we don't have to stay there!

No matter how hard he might have tried, Ezekiel would not have been able to cover the enormous quantity of bones in the valley. And neither can we. We must learn to speak to the low places in our lives, demanding depression and bitterness to leave. We also must command the gifts and talents lying dormant within us to come to life.

> *We must learn to speak to the low places in our lives, demanding depression and bitterness to leave. We also must command the gifts and talents lying dormant within us to come to life.*

Sometimes, God will lead you back to your valleys and low, dry places just to help you resurrect them. He will enable you to recall an experience or revisit areas of hurt and disappointments that are hindering you. God doesn't want you to be stuck or held back by anything your past. He doesn't want you dragging along anything that brings shame, pain, or unhappiness.

We can't ignore death or cover it up. But we can—and we must—replace it with life. We do this by speaking the Word of God with our mouths. God instructed Ezekiel to prophesy, which means to speak under the influence of God's divine Spirit. When Ezekiel opened his mouth in obedience to God, the words of his mouth created an atmosphere for the miraculous. Not only did God tell Ezekiel to prophesy, but He also gave him the specific words to say. The

> *Speaking the Word of God will cause flesh to come upon the dry, empty bones of your life.*

result was a powerful manifestation of an *"exceedingly great army."*

When a Spirit-filled individual speaks God's Word, she produces creative ability. Speaking the Word of God will cause flesh to come upon the dry, empty bones of your life.

God's Word accomplishes whatever it is sent to do, and it does not return void. Remember, our words are servants that we speak forth; they act and produce according to their nature. The prophet Isaiah related this concept as spoken by God Himself, saying, *"My word…that goes forth from My mouth…shall not return to Me void, but it shall accomplish what I please, and it shall prosper in the thing for which I sent it"* (Isaiah 55:11).

Speak fruitful words into your life. Say to your situation what God has said and let the sinews that were once dead become sensitive so that you can feel and move again. Many women have been wounded so deeply that they no longer feel in certain areas, but God is able to replenish their emotions and restore their wholeness, even in the driest valleys of their existence. His divine love for us resurrects any parts of us that have shriveled up and died; He quenches our spiritual thirst. He will envelop any of our dry, naked bones with skin so that our sensitive places can be covered and protected.

But this miraculous process must begin with our proclamation and affirmation of what He has said, for His words are spirit and life. They produce fruit wherever they are sent, even when spoken by human mouths, for God has promised their effectiveness. Jesus said, *"It is the Spirit who gives life; the flesh profits nothing. The words that I speak to you are spirit, and they are life"* (John 6:63).

When you speak God's Word, the supernatural will manifest. As with the bones in the valley with Ezekiel, there will be a noise and a rattling, and you soon will see your situation breathe new life, according to God's plans. After Ezekiel had spoken what God had commanded him to, the bones in the valley became a strong army. So, too, will the dry bones in your life breathe anew when you speak the Word of God.

20

FRUIT: THE FIBER OF LIFE

But the fruit of the Spirit is love, joy, peace, patience, kindness,
goodness, faithfulness, gentleness and self-control. Against such things
there is no law.
—Galatians 5:22–23 (NIV)

It's not always easy to exemplify the fruit when trying circumstances trigger your frustrations, tempt you to compromise your morals, or cloud your judgment. How, then, do you manage to display long-suffering, gentleness, and self-control in the face of adversity? You must have faith, for that's how the just and righteous live. (See Romans 1:17.) And you can't have faith without love and the other seven qualities (joy, peace, longsuffering, gentleness, goodness, temperance and meekness) that comprise the fruit of the spirit. It is as simple as that. So, instead of being overcome by the emotional drain that accompanies the perplexities of life, allow God's Spirit to minister peace to you. As you embrace the peace that surpasses all understanding, begin to allow the love of God to constrain you so that you will not respond in unbelief. Walk in faith. Add love to your faith, because faith works by love. Make declarations in accordance with God's Word. (See Romans 4:17.)

Every day, you face challenges that require you to use or refuse your fruit. When you purpose to walk daily in the fruit of the Spirit in every aspect of your life, it is likely that you will minister someone's healing, deliverance, or salvation. The good things that come from the fruit of the Spirit in your life aren't just for you; they're for others, too.

The peace of God, which surpasses understanding, will guard your hearts and minds through Christ Jesus. (Philippians 4:7)

How can we know that we have His Spirit? The fruit of the Spirit in our lives, which is demonstrated by godly responses to all situations, evidences the presence of His Spirit within us. As we allow our spirits to submit to His Spirit, we begin bearing the fruit thereof: love, joy, peace, patience, kindness, goodness, faithfulness, gentleness, and self-control. Even though there are nine distinct attributes that characterize the fruit of the Spirit, the Bible regards them all as one. For instance, love is an attribute that accompanies each fruit. You can't have one without the rest. All of the fruits complement their counterparts.

> *For every situation we face in life, there is a specific fruit of the Spirit that should shape and color our response.*

As we continue to develop into the fullness of the Godhead, the fiber of our fruit should reflect God's image and likeness. What we're "made of" will be evident in our conversations, our relationships, our actions, and our lives. The fabric of who we are should minister to other people, who should never have to see the garments of our characters unravel and come apart when we're confronted by trouble or experiencing pressure. If we are being persecuted, patience, or longsuffering, should adorn us. When calamity befalls us, we should be wearing peace. For every situation we face in life, there is a specific fruit of the Spirit that should shape and color our response.

The Fruit of Love

If I speak in the tongues of men and of angels, but have not love, I am only a resounding gong or a clanging cymbal. If I have the gift of prophecy and can fathom all mysteries and all knowledge, and if I have a faith that can move mountains, but have not love, I am nothing. If I give all I possess to the poor and surrender my body to the flames, but have not love, I gain nothing. Love is patient, love is kind. It does not envy, it does not boast, it is not proud. It is not rude, it is not self-seeking, it is not easily angered, it keeps no record of wrongs. Love does not delight in evil but rejoices with the truth. It always protects, always trusts, always hopes, always perseveres. Love never fails. But where there are prophecies, they will cease; where there are tongues, they will be stilled; where there is knowledge, it will pass away. For we know in part and we prophesy in part, but when perfection comes, the imperfect disappears. When I was a child, I talked like a child, I thought like a child, I reasoned like a child. When I became a man, I put childish ways behind me. Now we see but a poor reflection as in a mirror; then we shall see face to face. Now I know in part; then I shall know fully, even as I am fully known. And now these three remain: faith, hope and love. But the greatest of these is love. (1 Corinthians 13:1–13 NIV)

Paul took up the same theme in the book of Romans, saying,

Owe no one anything except to love one another, for he who loves another has fulfilled the law. For the commandments, "You shall not commit adultery," "You shall not murder," "You shall not steal," "You shall not bear false witness," "You shall not covet," and if there is any other commandment, are all summed up in this saying, namely, "You shall love your neighbor as yourself." Love does no harm to a neighbor; therefore love is the fulfillment of the law. (Romans 13:8–10)

If we love our neighbors, we will do no wrong to them. When we're acting in love, we will not lie, cheat, covet, steal, or do any such thing. Purpose to walk in love and do the Word, because the Word works! Love never fails!

> *If we love our neighbors, we will do no wrong to them.*

God is love, according to 1 John 4:8, and love is the highest manifestation of the personality of God in the earth. Because He loved us, God sent His only Son to redeem us from the clutches of Satan. When we give our lives to Jesus, God pours His love into our hearts through His Holy Spirit, whom we receive. "*Now hope does not disappoint, because the love of God has been poured out in our hearts by the Holy Spirit who was given to us*" (Romans 5:5).

Because of His love in us, we have the ability to love others, and we can love them just as God loves.

> *One [Pharisee], a lawyer, asked [Jesus] a question, testing Him, and saying, "Teacher, which is the great commandment in the law?" Jesus said to him, "'You shall love the LORD your God with all your heart, with all your soul, and with all your mind.' This is the first and great commandment. And the second is like it: 'You shall love your neighbor as yourself.' On these two commandments hang all the Law and the Prophets."* (Matthew 22:35–40)

God desires us to walk harmoniously with one another. God expects us to love Him, but He also wants us to love one another. Galatians 5:14 tells us, *"For all the law is fulfilled in one word, even in this: 'You shall love your neighbor as yourself.'"*

It's vitally important that we live in a way that constantly releases God's love to others. Jesus said that the world will recognize that we belong to Christ by the love that we express to one another: *"By this all will know that you are My disciples, if you have love for one another"* (John 13:35).

> *The key indicator of a Christian's level of spiritual maturity is her love.*

So powerful is the love of God within us that it causes us to walk peacefully in situations that would generally cause chaos and anxiety. The key indicator of a Christian's level of spiritual maturity is her love. Claiming to be a Christian and failing to walk in the fruit of love causes us to be false witnesses. Love is what must distinguish Christians.

God's love, which is called *agape* in Greek, is supernatural, and it goes beyond our emotions. Natural, human love is often self-centered, and it's generally based on a system of exchange: we must receive love in order to give love. God's love is completely unconditional, immeasurable and unfailing.

Conditional love keeps track of wrongs and tends to hold grudges, but unconditional love keeps no record of wrong, nor is it self-seeking. (See 1 Corinthians 13:5 NIV.) Jesus made this point in His Sermon on the Mount:

> *But if you love those who love you, what credit is that to you? For even sinners love those who love them. And if you do good to those who do good to you, what credit is that to you? For even sinners do the same....*

But love your enemies, do good…hoping for nothing in return; and your reward will be great, and you will be sons of the Most High. For He is kind to the unfaithful and evil. (Luke 6:32–33, 35)

When you choose to love someone who has done you wrong, it is because the love of God in you gives you the ability. It's extremely difficult to love someone who has hurt you without relying on divine love. On our own, we can't overcome the instinct to seek revenge. This is precisely why God wants us to yield to His love, for it gives us the grace and ability to love the unlovable.

For the Christian, walking in love is not optional—it's required. The true test of spiritual maturity is not how long you can pray or how often you read your Bible but how you love others.

Allowing the love of God to operate in your life will bring great blessings to those around you. Love is the most powerful force on earth. According to 1 Corinthians 13:7, love endures everything without weakening. Love will never fail you; people may, but love never will. No matter what happens, trust in God's love, because it is able to withstand the strongest of storms and restore shattered lives. When we learn as women to believe in the love of God that resides within us, that love will always cause us to win and overcome in life. *"And now these three remain: faith, hope and love. But the greatest of these is love"* (1 Corinthians 13:13 NIV).

The Power of Peace

But the wisdom that is from above is first pure, then peaceable, gentle, and easy to be entreated, full of mercy and good fruits, without partiality, and without hypocrisy. And the fruit of righteousness is sown in peace of them that make peace. (James 3:17–18 KJV)

Peace is not just the absence of noise and is more than a soothing or tranquil feeling. It's a state of being and a place of authority, power, and order. When something is chaotic, there is usually an absence of peace. But when peace comes, order follows. In the legal system, the person designated as the justice of the peace holds a position of authority and has been mandated to bring order and peace.

We are told in John 14:27 that Jesus has given us His peace, and in Galatians 5:22–23, we understand that peace is a fruit of the Spirit that is resident within us. Sometimes, we take peace for granted; we fail to place value on its worth. But peace is essential because it exemplifies a place of rest and trust in God. Psalm 119:165 gives us these words of comfort: *"Great peace have they which love thy law: and nothing shall offend them"* (KJV).

Peace causes things to come into place, and God allowed us to have His supernatural peace so that we can bring things in order. Satan's desire, however, is to disturb and disrupt our peace as women. He wants to plant his seed of influence in our lives. The Bible states that the seed of a woman was going to be against the enemy's seed. (See Genesis 3:15.) Biologically speaking, a woman doesn't have seed. Men are the producers of seed and women are the incubators. The seed fertilizes the woman's egg, and she carries the growing offspring, eventually giving birth to a new life.

The *"offspring"* (NIV) or *"seed"* (NKJV, KJV, NASB) referred to in Genesis 3:15 is Jesus, the Seed of Mary, a woman. This verse was a prophetic picture of a spiritual seed. Instead of walking in peace, Satan wants us to carry his seed so that we will give birth to his thoughts, ideas, and suggestions. Peace comes from the Hebrew word *shalom,* which means "prosperity." According to Galatians 3:16, we are the seed of Abraham. God promised that all of Abraham's seed would live under a blessing. I'm blessed because I am of Abraham and I have within me the peace and prosperity that God gave to Abraham. As Abraham's seed, I am an inheritor of his blessing; his prosperity and his peace belong to me.

> *God promised us that in troubled times, He would give us a peace that surpasses all understanding.*

We carry the seed of God. We can't allow the enemy to cause us to give birth to things that will destroy our lives. God promised us that in troubled times, He would give us a peace that surpasses all understanding. (See Philippians 4:7.) Circumstances come into our lives to disturb our peace and steal our joy. Joy is an expression! Peace is a possession! When the enemy comes, he comes to take us out of that place of authority and into a place of inferiority, where we are subject to the deeds and workings of the flesh. Therefore, we must stand strong in the power of God's might and resist the devil's temptations.

When it comes to overcoming, according to God's Word, you've already won! The blows of the devil don't mean anything when it's time to fight because we *"fight the good fight of faith"* (1 Timothy 6:12). A fight is good only when you're winning, and we've already won, thanks to Christ Jesus!

Women Are Winners

God has always used women to accomplish His will on the earth. The Bible says that Eve's seed will conquer the enemy and will crush his head. (See Genesis 3:15 NIV.) She will crush him under her feet, and so will you. Realize you've already won. When your ways please God, He will make your enemies be at peace with you, at the same time giving you His peace that surpasses understanding.

> *When your ways please God, He will make your enemies be at peace with you, at the same time giving you His peace that surpasses understanding.*

Fighting like a girl seems more advantageous than fighting like a boy. In her book *Fight Like a Girl*, Lisa Bevere brings attention to this fact. When you fight like a girl, there's no telling where you're going to hit and what impact your punch will produce. Boys tend to be more prepared. They square up, put up their dukes, and know where they plan to execute their punch. Therefore, you can predict where their punch will come from and thereby block or guard it. Most girls aren't like that! A girl winds up like a windmill. You may receive a blow to the head or a kick in the shin and may lose some hair when fighting with a girl!

The person on the receiving end will wind up in bad shape! Although the fight may not seem strategic, girls always seem to get the job done.

We understand that the weapons of our warfare are not carnal but mighty through God! (See 2 Corinthians 10:4.) Satan can strike with his best shot, but when you have the peace of God, you can *"stand firm"* and *"let nothing move you"* (1 Corinthians 15:58 NIV).

The book of Judges includes a story about King Abimelech, who was infamous for burning and destroying the villages of the people of Israel. The men of Israel did nothing about it. But there was a woman—a widow—who got fed up with his destructive habits. When she heard that the king and his men were on their way to her village, she devised a plan. Sure enough, Abimelech and his servants arrived. Seeing that no one else was doing anything to stop them, this woman got a millstone and dropped it out of a window on Abimelech's head, cracking his skull and bringing an end to his reign of terror. Her actions brought peace to her entire village. *Fighting like a girl is a powerful thing!*

> *As a woman, when you have the peace of God, you are determined to see Satan's defeat. You don't care who gets the credit as long as the enemy is destroyed!*

When Abimelech realized he was going to die, he told his servant to slay him with his sword because he didn't want it ever to be said that a woman had destroyed him. So, the servant acted at the behest of the king and slew him. (See Judges 9:53–56.)

As a woman, when you have the peace of God, you are determined to see Satan's defeat. You don't care who gets the credit as long as the enemy is destroyed! This widow was a woman who knew who she was—and whose she was!

When you can come into an out-of-control situation and bring peace, that's God working through you. Things will come from the outside to disturb your peace, so you must never forget that God has given you His authority. You must dwell in the place of peace. As Jesus said in Matthew 5:9, *"Blessed are the peacemakers, for they shall be called sons [and daughters] of God."*

Jesus is the Justice of our peace. He brings judgment. Command your peace to remain and allow God to use you. Allow the perfect peace of God to rule you. The Bible encourages us to shod our feet with the preparation of the gospel of peace (see Ephesians 6:15) so that, wherever we go, we take the peace of Christ with us. *"Now may the Lord of peace Himself give you peace always in every way. The Lord be with you all"* (2 Thessalonians 3:16).

A Prayer for Peace

Father,

We thank You for Your peace, which passes understanding. We thank You for making it available to us so that we can use it to find comfort and strength in times of adversity. Thank You that when the enemy comes in like a flood, You lift a standard against him and bring to us Your perpetual peace. Thank You that we are not consumed by perplexities or overcome by challenges we face in life. We find comfort in the peace You provide to us daily. Your mercies are new every morning, and because we love Your law, we have great peace so that nothing will offend us. Thank You for Your peace, Father. In Jesus' name, amen.

21

UNFORGIVENESS IS NOT A WORD

D id you know that *unforgiveness* is not really a word? There is no definition to substantiate it. Despite its prevalence in discussions on the importance of practicing forgiveness, as opposed to its antithesis, the spell check function on my computer did not recognize the word as I was writing this book. Moreover, the Bible doesn't use it. So, if it isn't in the dictionary, the Bible, or the lexicon in Microsoft Word, why does the body of Christ spend so much time walking in it?

If the blood of Jesus can save us from our sins, those of us who have received the gift of salvation should comprehend the grace of being forgiven by a sinless Savior for sins that would condemn us to death. How much more, then, should we forgive the comparatively minor offenses our brothers and sisters commit against us? Jesus said to His disciples, *"If you forgive men their trespasses, your heavenly Father will also forgive you. But if you do not forgive men their trespasses, neither will your Father forgive your trespasses"* (Matthew 6:14–15).

Jesus warned His disciples, *"It is impossible that no offenses should come, but woe to him through whom they do come!"* (Luke 17:1). We experience offenses when other people speak or act against us, bringing hurt or shame. But the offenses we often let govern our thoughts are ones of blame or fault for something someone said or how we "felt" he or she treated us.

When you refuse to forgive or to settle an offense, it is an act of rebellion against God's Word, which admonishes us, *"'Be angry, and do not sin': do not let the sun go down on your wrath"* (Ephesians 4:26).

When Peter asked Jesus, *"Lord, how often shall my brother sin against me, and I forgive him? Up to seven times?"* Jesus responded, *"I do not say to you, up to seven times, but up to seventy times seven"* (Matthew 18:21–22). Jesus ended this lesson with the account of a ruler who required restitution of his servant. When that servant begged for mercy, his master forgave him. Then, the same servant went to his fellow servant and demanded repayment of a debt, but when the fellow servant begged for mercy, the other refused to grant him pardon, even though he himself had just been cleared of a debt that was much greater. He had his fellow servant thrown in jail until he was able to pay his debt. When his master learned what he had done, he called him "wicked" and had him tortured and thrown in jail, as well, until the debt was paid, all because he was unwilling to forgive. (See Matthew 18:23–34.)

One of the best examples of forgiveness I've heard is that of Shellie R. Warren in her article "Forgiveness: It's for You…Not for Them."[3] Having suffered various hardships throughout her lifetime, including physical and sexual abuse, she struggled with Jesus' command to forgive *"seventy times seven"* times. She did the math and wrote in her journal, "490 times? How could *anyone* forgive someone *that* much?" It didn't take her long to reach the startling realization that if she had to forgive someone that many times, then it must be for her benefit, not for the benefit of her offender. Warren explained that forgiveness "is not denying that something bad happened. Instead, forgiveness prevents the deed from doing any further damage than it already has to you and your world."

Forgiveness Brings Health and Healing

Indeed, forgiving others brings health benefits to our bodies. Warren refers to a book by Robert D. Enright, *Forgiveness Is a Choice: A Step-by-Step Process for Resolving Anger and Restoring Hope*, which explores the link between forgiveness and health, and specifically the power of forgiveness to break cycles of bitterness, resentment, and wrath. Moreover, forgiveness may reduce hypertension and lower blood pressure, putting individuals at

---

[3] Shellie R. Warren, "Forgiveness: It's for You…Not for Them," LifeScript.com (20 June 2008). http://www.lifescript.com/Soul/Self/Growth/The_Gift_of_forgiveness.aspx

a lower risk for cardiovascular problems, according to research performed by Dr. Fred Luskin, director of the Stanford Forgiveness Projects.[4]

Though forgiveness is not a fruit of the Spirit, it is definitely a characteristic of the fruit—love, peace, and patience, in particular. When the love of God has been shed abroad in your heart, then you understand why you should forgive, even when your flesh resists.

> *When the love of God has been shed abroad in your heart, then you understand why you should forgive, even when your flesh resists.*

A key component of extending forgiveness is learning to do as the apostle Paul did: *"Forgetting those things which are behind and reaching forward to those things which are ahead, I press on toward the goal for the prize of the upward call of God in Christ Jesus"* (Philippians 3:13–14). When you forgive someone, your emotions are no longer tied to the act that was committed against you. But if you find yourself still harboring hurt feelings and overwhelming emotions, this indicates that you probably haven't forgiven the individual completely. Guarding your heart or being sensitive when you're in the presence of the individual who hurt you may be evidence that you should check your heart. It is always a good practice to perform regular "love checkups."

I use Paul's words to define *forgiveness*: *"forgetting those things which are behind;"* remembering an offense no more; becoming free. When we choose to forgive, we set free not only ourselves, but also the person who hurt us. Everything God has given to us has been freely given. Why should we entrap ourselves in the refusal to forgive and make everybody pay for what they've done to us? God wants us all to walk in the liberty by which He has made us *all* free!

Forgiveness: The End of Blame

The opposite of *forgiveness* might include *blame*, which can prove harmful if we hold on to it for too long. It isn't our responsibility to make others pay for the sins they commit against us. God is our Avenger. *"'Vengeance*

---

[4] Fred Luskin et al., "Hypertension Reduction through Forgiveness Training," *Journal of Pastoral Care and Counseling* 60, no. 1–2 (2006): 27.

is Mine, I will repay,' says the Lord" (Romans 12:19). In the same chapter, Paul instructed us, "*Do not be overcome by evil, but overcome evil with good*" (verse 21).

Again, our body language speaks volumes, especially when it comes to forgiveness. You may be able to say that you've forgiven someone—nothing's wrong, you've moved on—but what you do afterward speaks more loudly than what you've said. As we discussed earlier, our nonverbal communication conveys our thoughts and feelings. Throughout the body of Christ, too many people are holding on to hurt, offense, and rejection much longer than they ought to.

> *You may be able to say that you've forgiven someone—nothing's wrong, you've moved on—but what you do afterward speaks more loudly than what you've said.*

Years ago, there was a point at which I was counseling so many hurting people that I suggested to our church's administrative staff, "I want to host a service for hurting people." After I had made this suggestion, I realized that there wasn't a facility large enough to accommodate all the people who would attend. Is there any place to lay down the hurt? Or perhaps a more effective question would be, are we *willing* to lay the hurt down?

It is time to move on and stop harboring unforgiving dispositions. Withholding forgiveness is not in God's plan, and unforgiveness is not in His Word. God wants us to forgive because He wants us free from the bondage of not forgiving. Refusing to forgive will hinder our spiritual growth, and, as we have seen, it can adversely affect our health. Don't allow your thoughts to give way to actions that contradict God's Word. Never *react* to anything; instead, put God's Word into action. Take the initiative to forgive, and you won't be ruled by the harmful words and actions of others.

I once counseled a woman who told me that she had forgiven her husband, but every time he went somewhere without her, she assumed that he was falling back into his old habits. Prior to our counseling, the couple had been separated, and she had threatened to leave him for good. Now, she was repeating those threats based on what things looked like to her.

If she had never had a problem with her husband, she would not have doubted him and imagined the worst whenever he went out alone. The memory of what he had done was holding her captive. But as she exchanged her thoughts for the Word of God and spent time meditating on its truths, the Holy Spirit showed her that what she was imagining wasn't her husband's intent at all.

Once she realized what was preventing her from forgiving her husband, she began to cast down the thoughts of her imagination, and then she examined herself. Finally, she forgave him, truly and completely, and the mercy that God had made available to her was extended to her husband, as well.

Relationships are among the most vital aspects of our lives. They must be healthy; they've got to be whole. We must not allow negative thinking to cause us to abandon our marriages, friendships, and other relationships because strife has entered our minds due to a refusal to forgive. Don't entertain negative thoughts or troubling assumptions about others, for these will only hinder your growth and keep you from enjoying fruitful relationships. If your supervisor overlooks you for a promotion, don't allow resentment and bitterness to lodge in your heart. Purpose not to allow an unforgiving, relentless disposition to govern you, for it will only hurt you.

> *Don't entertain negative thoughts or troubling assumptions about others, for these will only hinder your growth and keep you from enjoying fruitful relationships.*

Today, take inventory of your thought life. Check your heart; check your fruit. Peruse your address book, read through your e-mails, and examine your thoughts and feelings. If a certain name sticks out like a sore thumb, or if you feel a pang, it's likely that you need to allow God to complete a work of grace in you. Allow Him to heal you so you'll be able to forgive—totally and completely.

Let my prayer minister to you:

Father, I thank You for giving to us Your only Son, Jesus, who, by dying on the cross, paid the price for our sins. Thank You for pardoning us and for making us Your righteousness through Him.

Thank You that the old things have passed away and that all things have become new. Thank You that because we have been forgiven, we, too, have the power to forgive.

I pray for every person reading this book who has unresolved strife in her heart. I pray that You would cause each one to be released from the pain that has caused her to be unforgiving. I pray that the love of Jesus Christ would envelop her and constrain her from walking in strife and an unforgiving spirit.

Show her the condition of her heart and enable her to judge herself and others by Your Word, not by human words or actions. Give her Your peace, which surpasses understanding, and grant her the desire to be released from everything that would hinder her spiritual growth and emotional maturity.

I pray that she will take captive every thought, suggestion, or influence that would keep her from receiving Your Word, which is able to change her soul and cleanse her from all unrighteousness. Teach her to walk in Your love and to extend it to everyone, including those who have hurt her with an offense, whether real or imagined. Give her the ability to cast down every imagination that exalts itself against Your knowledge, and show her how to take all her thoughts captive and make them obedient to Christ! In Jesus' name, amen.

22
FIND YOUR HEART

My son Brandon recently ministered a powerful message that paralleled what I was working on in this portion of the book. His artful articulation was so detailed yet simple that I asked him to expound upon his message in written form. It follows in this chapter.

Treasure Hunt: Find Your Heart

*Do not lay up for yourselves treasures on earth, where moth and rust destroy and where thieves break in and steal; but lay up for yourselves treasures in heaven, where neither moth nor rust destroys and where thieves do not break in and steal. **For where your treasure is, there your heart will be also.*** (Matthew 6:19–21, emphasis added)

God wants the best for us, both in this life and in the next. In order to receive what God has for us, including salvation, we have to be willing to change. And this change must start with our hearts. Our hearts are where we store our emotions, our passions (desires), and our wills. We have to be willing to give God our hearts.

The Bible makes this clear to us in the tenth chapter of Mark. A wealthy young man came and knelt before Jesus and asked how he could inherit eternal life. Jesus responded with a question, asking him whether he knew the commandments. The rich young ruler responded affirmatively, saying that he had kept the commandments from his youth, but Jesus told him that something was still lacking. (See Mark 10:17–23.)

I found this interesting, because in John 14:15, Jesus said, *"If you love Me, you will keep My commandments"* (NASB). So, it seems like the man loved Jesus, because he was keeping the commandments. Why, then, was he still lacking what was necessary for eternal life? I realized that following the commandments meant keeping Jewish law, just as the Ten Commandments were *the law* in my parents' home. There were severe consequences for breaking the law.

> *Knowledge of the consequences of doing wrong is one thing; walking in righteousness, however, is a personal decision and a matter of the heart.*

But just because we practice the law doesn't mean that God has our hearts. The young man in Mark 10 may have kept the commandments because of the law. Knowledge of the consequences of doing wrong is one thing; walking in righteousness, however, is a personal decision and a matter of the heart. *Though God requires us to live right, right living must start with the heart.*

In our efforts to avoid wrong, we fail to give God our hearts. We try to find out what we can get away with. As Jesus said in John 5:39–40, *"You search the Scriptures, because you think that in them you have eternal life; and it is these that bear witness of Me; and you are unwilling to come to Me, that you may have life"* (NASB).

Jesus told the rich man to sell all of his possessions, give the money to the poor, take up his cross, and follow Him. But the man turned away with sorrow because he had great possessions. Note that even with great possessions, he was full of sorrow!

In Proverbs 10:22, we are reminded that *"the blessing of the LORD makes one rich, and He adds no sorrow with it."* The young man in Mark 10 didn't receive the blessing because something was missing—his heart. Though the rich man followed the commandments, his heart was with his money instead of with God. He wasn't willing to give up what was valuable to him. His treasure was his wealth and possessions, so that's where his heart was, in accordance with Matthew 6:21.

Give God Your Heart

We give God our hearts by letting Him know that He is our treasure. He's valuable to us! How do we accomplish this? The same way we give our loved ones access to our hearts: we share what is valuable to us, such as time, money, and resources. The same principles apply in our relationships with God.

Give God what you value. God wants to know that you are willing to give those treasured things to Him. That is how we let Him know He has our hearts. Remember, if it doesn't mean anything to you, it won't mean anything to God. God gave us His most prized possession: His Son, Jesus Christ. As you seek Him above all things, the desires of your heart will be added to you, as well. (See Matthew 6:33.) His Word promises it. So, give God what you value. Give Him your heart!

> *As you seek God above all things, the desires of your heart will be added to you, as well.*

Jesus desired for this man to be a part of the kingdom, and He perceived that his treasures—his wealth and possessions—were the obstacle that would keep him from receiving eternal life. In Mark 10:25, Jesus told His disciples that as difficult as it is for a camel to pass through *"the eye of a needle"* (a very narrow gate), that's how difficult it is for the rich to inherit eternal life—not because of their riches, but because of their hearts, which pursue their misplaced treasures.

We are therefore admonished to seek God's kingdom and His righteous; when we do so, the God-given desires of our hearts will be granted to us, as well. We have this promise in Luke 12:23–34:

> *Life is more than food, and the body is more than clothing. Consider the ravens, for they neither sow nor reap, which have neither storehouse nor barn; and God feeds them. Of how much more value are you than the birds? And which of you by worrying can add one cubit to his stature? If you then are not able to do the least, why are you anxious for the rest? Consider the lilies, how they grow: they neither toil nor spin; and yet I say to you, even Solomon in all his glory was not arrayed like one of*

these. If then God so clothes the grass, which today is in the field and tomorrow is thrown into the oven, how much more will He clothe you, O you of little faith? And do not seek what you should eat or what you should drink, nor have an anxious mind. For all these things the nations of the world seek after, and your Father knows that you need these things. But seek the kingdom of God, and all these things shall be added to you. Do not fear, little flock, for it is your Father's good pleasure to give you the kingdom. Sell what you have and give alms; provide yourselves money bags which do not grow old, a treasure in the heavens that does not fail, where no thief approaches nor moth destroys. For where your treasure is, there your heart will be also.

CONCLUSION: THE VIRTUOUS WOMAN

Who can find a virtuous woman? for her price is far above rubies. The heart of her husband doth safely trust in her, so that he shall have no need of spoil. She will do him good and not evil all the days of her life. She seeketh wool, and flax, and worketh willingly with her hands. She is like the merchants' ships; she bringeth her food from afar. She riseth also while it is yet night, and giveth meat to her household, and a portion to her maidens. She considereth a field, and buyeth it: with the fruit of her hands she planteth a vineyard. She girdeth her loins with strength, and strengtheneth her arms. She perceiveth that her merchandise is good: her candle goeth not out by night. She layeth her hands to the spindle, and her hands hold the distaff. She stretcheth out her hand to the poor; yea, she reacheth forth her hands to the needy. She is not afraid of the snow for her household: for all her household are clothed with scarlet. She maketh herself coverings of tapestry; her clothing is silk and purple. Her husband is known in the gates, when he sitteth among the elders of the land. She maketh fine linen, and selleth it; and delivereth girdles unto the merchant. Strength and honour are her clothing; and she shall rejoice in time to come. She openeth her mouth with wisdom; and in her tongue is the law of kindness. She looketh well to the ways of her household, and eateth not the bread of idleness. Her children arise up, and call her blessed; her husband also, and he praiseth her. Many daughters have done virtuously, but thou excellest them all. Favour is deceitful, and beauty is vain: but a woman that feareth the LORD, she shall be praised. Give her of the fruit of her hands; and let her own works praise her in the gates.

—Proverbs 31:10–31 (KJV)

While every woman has a unique fabric that makes up her being, there is a common thread that is to unite all of our fabrics—the thread of virtue. Proverbs 31 describes the virtuous woman, asking who can find her (see Proverbs 31:10), which means that virtuous women are in high demand.

Few women exhibit the character, strength, and poise of this biblical example. She is a businesswoman, a world traveler, a minister, a designer, an interior decorator, a confidante, a wife, a mother, and an exquisite lady overall.

The greatest thing about the virtuous woman is that you have the potential to exhibit the same qualities—you can be the virtuous woman! When God formed you in your mother's womb, He endued you with great worth. Your unique creativity, ingenuity, and vitality are gifts from God that He desires you to use in His kingdom. Like different fabrics especially suited for specific circumstances—spandex for athletics, wool for winter sweaters, Lycra for bathing suits, and satin for elegant gowns—every woman has a gift, talent, or ability given to her by God to be used for the kingdom and for His glory. Rise out of obscurity and capitalize on what God has invested in you! Pursue the passions that bring you pleasure and peace.

As never before, God is raising women who will hold high the standard of righteousness and minister to the world with the talents and abilities God has given them. If you have an idea, a concept, or a vision that you've been dreaming of for some time, don't allow the enemy to hinder you any longer. Your gift has the power to bring healing and increase to your house and to those to whom you minister. Use your gift to help others, whether it's researching a new treatment for breast cancer or something else. Whatever God has placed in you to do, *do!*

A Virtuous Woman's Confession

Father, I thank You that I am a virtuous woman, more precious than jewels.

I select the best and work with willing hands; I am like the merchant ships, bringing needed provision.

I arise while it is still night and provide food for my household, and portions for those who help me.

I evaluate good investments and move wisely as I am led, bringing continual increase into my household.

I draw upon my inner strength; my arms are strong in the Lord.

I can see that the fruit of my work is good, and my lamp never goes out at night because I always work to produce more in the lives of my family members.

I am not afraid of hard work, and I extend my hands to the poor and needy.

I am not afraid when the seasons of life change, because everyone in my household has his need met.

I am creative and wise, and I wear the finest of clothing.

I am strong in business and produce powerful results because strength and honor are my clothing. I am optimistic about the future.

My mouth opens with wisdom, and loving instruction is on my tongue.

I watch over the activities of my household, and I am never idle.

My children rise up and call me blessed, and my husband praises me.

Many women are capable, but I surpass them all!

Charm is deceptive and beauty is fleeting, but I am a woman who fears the Lord, and I am praised.

I receive the reward of my labor, and my life is respected throughout the city.

In Jesus' name, amen.

ABOUT THE AUTHOR

The ministry of Pamela M. Hines began in 1982 following the miraculous raising to life of her husband, Darrell L. Hines, after he was tragically struck by lightning.

Together, they pastor one of the most dynamic churches in Milwaukee and are the overseeing founders of several other Christian Faith Fellowship Churches. Pamela is the cofounder of Dominion Fellowship, an outreach ministry encompassing a diversity of races and religious backgrounds that caters to the specific needs of husband-and-wife ministry teams.

Pamela has an anointing upon her life to minister to women. She is the founder of the Women's Image Course, a powerful series of lessons designed to meet the needs of women. Her grace and message attract women from a variety of racial, economic, and social backgrounds. Her aim is to empower women to be all that God has called them to be, focusing on the spirit, soul, and body. Pamela's earnest desire is to help the body of Christ walk in the knowledge and authority that God has given to them and to strengthen its members through the ministry of God's Word.

Her message is practical, and those who hear her will be challenged to become all that God desires them to be.